A FIRST GUIDE TO
FISHING
STAN PIECHA

**Published by Ring Publications Ltd.,
1-3 Wine Office Court, Fleet Street, London EC4A 3AL.**

Design by New Openings Design Group.
Illustrations on page 20, 21, 76 & 77 by David Nunn.
Photographs supplied by Mike Millman, Bill Howes, Shakespeare Co.,
Daiwa, Angling Times, Stan Piecha, Marks & Marlow.
Filmset by SX Composing Ltd., Rayleigh, Essex.
Reproduction by Web Offset Reproductions Ltd., London.
Printed in England by Ambassador College Press, St. Albans, Herts.
Bound in England by Pitman Press Ltd., Bath, Avon.

Contents

Introduction   4

Chapter One   Coarse fishing – starting from scratch   6

Chapter Two   Coarse baits – all the essentials and how to breed maggots   12

Chapter Three   Know your coarse fish – identification, habits, locations and baits preferred   18

Chapter Four   How to catch your first fish   24

Chapter Five   Reading a water – finding the habitats of fish   30

Chapter Six   Float fishing – a step-by-step guide   32

Chapter Seven   Leger fishing – a step-by-step guide   36

Chapter Eight   Pike fishing – a step-by-step guide   40

Chapter Nine   Trout fishing – a step-by-step guide   44

Chapter Ten   Canals and small stream fishing – how to get the best from these small waters   48

Chapter Eleven   Sea fishing – equipment needed for shore and boat   52

Chapter Twelve   Sea baits – collect your own   64

Chapter Thirteen   Know your sea fish – identification, habits, locations and baits preferred   72

Chapter Fourteen   Habitats of sea fish – where to fish and likely spots to look for   80

Introduction

Fishing is fun and it would be fair to say that the more you catch, the more pleasure can be had from the sport. Obviously it would become monotonous to guarantee a bulging keepnet each time you visited a water. The enjoyment would be taken away if you knew that you were going to strike it rich each time.

For it's the mystery of fishing – never knowing quite what you are going to hook – that makes it so appealing to millions of people in Britain.

You could go to a water where you normally catch only small roach and land a big carp completely out of the blue. A day's beachcasting from the shore for flat-fish could come up with a record bass. You never know.

Everyone has bad days when, no matter what you try, it is impossible to tempt even the small fry on to your hook. These days make the good ones that more memorable and pleasurable.

But many anglers – young and old, beginners and ones who have been involved with the sport for years – have more than their share of blank periods. The reason is simple. They have never bothered learning the basics of the sport.

As with any pastime, the basic skills – and you do need skill to catch fish regularly – have to be learned and mastered. The days when fishing could be carried out with a bent pin, a piece of string and an old garden cane, are long gone.

Look into any tackle shop window and you will see an array of gear – rods, reels, hooks, lines, shot, and so on. For each one there are many more variations. One rod may suit carp fishing but will be unsuitable for general coarse fishing; fine wire hooks are fine for roach fishing but out of the question when trying to tackle tench.

And even when you have bought your tackle, then you have to set it up, plumb the depth, shot your float or, if you are fishing in the sea, you have to decide which weight to use, how far to cast, how should the hooks be spaced. The questions are endless and even when you have grasped the rudiments new problems are continually cropping up.

So as you can see it is impossible to start a successful fishing career on your own, no matter how old you are. Everyone has to be given a start and once that has been done you can put your own thoughts into fishing. You may develop better ways of making a certain float or preparing your bait.

I feel that all the subjects covered in The First Guide to Fishing will act as a stepping stone for any newcomer to the sport. I have tried to cover all aspects of fishing – sea, coarse and game – as deeply as possible.

While preparing each chapter I cast my mind back to the posers I was presented with. Many of them, like mixing groundbait or even casting, are now second nature but at the time they presented some real obstacles. By digesting the words contained in this book you will overcome the early hurdles. But it will not make you an instant expert – no book can do that. The only thing that can make you a complete and capable angler is practice, although short cuts can be made if you are armed with valuable background information from the start. Begin on the right lines and you will go on with increasing success.

Throughout this book I have given general guidelines for all branches of the sport. They are proven methods. The baits I have mentioned are the most common ones which I, and most successful anglers, have used.

However, as time goes on, you may find certain baits work better than others on your local water. It is up to you to experiment with baits and tactics so as to get the most from your fishing. Fish in lakes will often respond differently to those found in rivers – and even the feeding habits of river fish change, depending on whether the river is fast moving or slow.

On each outing try to think like a fish. If I was a roach living in this stretch of the river where would I want to live? In a featureless length or one with plenty of cover such as overhanging trees and bushes? The answer has to be the latter.

Also get tips from anglers who are successful in your area. Watch how they fish and find out why. They may be able to give you first-hand information to improve your catches.

But remember that no-one knows it all. When you stop listening, and reading about fishing – you stop learning.

CHAPTER ONE

Coarse fishing - starting from scratch

The days when a length of cane and a bent pin tied to a piece of string would catch fish are gone. Nowadays to go coarse fishing – which means catching fish such as roach, perch and bream from freshwater – you need the right tackle. Coarse fishing is the most popular branch of angling but also the most complicated.

Walk into any tackle shop for the first time and you will be confronted by an arsenal of fishing rods and reels. The choice is enormous but also critical. You must pick the right tackle to increase the odds of catching your first fish. So let us deal with each item needed.

Rods: Stay well clear of the "package deals". Some manufacturers advertise cheap "complete" beginners' outfits. They are eye catching but not fish catching. The rods are usually six foot models which may seem long enough to a novice but are much too restrictive for freshwater fishing.

The short rod will handicap the beginner from the start especially when trying to master the two essentials – casting and striking (setting a hook into a fish's mouth after a bite).

Summer on a picturesque lake and this young angler is waiting for his first bite.

There is no such thing as an all purpose coarse fishing rod. There are a multitude of rods on the market, many specifically made for things such as carp fishing, legering, spinning, or for use with a swimfeeder (to be dealt with later). If one rod is all that can be afforded then it MUST be a float rod of 12ft in length. Float fishing is the most enjoyable aspect of coarse fishing. The sight of a float bobbing about on the surface creates an exciting air of anticipation.

This may seem very long but the hollow glass fibre material used for most of today's rods is extremely light. Beginners aged from eight years upwards will be able to cope with rods of this length comfortably all day.

Now the field has been narrowed down, what sort of 12ft rod do you need? This is very much dictated by your pocket. Ideally you need one which has a tip action (a fairly soft top). This will make sure you feel the movements of even the tiniest fish hooked and therefore enjoy the skill of hooking a fish.

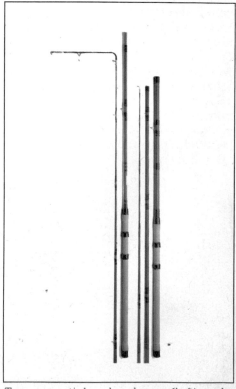

Two essential rods – leger (left) and float.

It needs to feel comfortable to handle. If the rod's handle is too long for your liking, pick one with a shorter handle. Take a tackle dealer's advice but always remember it is you who will have to fish with the equipment, so pick the rod which feels best. The only other piece of advice I can give in selecting your first rod is to make sure it has plenty of stand-off rings attached to it. A 12 footer should have about 11 rings on it – with most concentrated on the top joint. Rods of this size should be either three or four piece models.

Reels: Now you have chosen a good rod you need a decent reel to partner it. The two most common models are fixed spool and closed face reels. The fixed spool is the one I would recommend. Again go for one which is the most expensive in your price range. Make sure that it is made by a well-known firm, that it is smooth running when the handle is turned, that extra spools (which hold the line) can be bought and that spares are easily obtainable. If you are left-handed point this out to the tackle dealer for you will require a reel with a handle on the right-hand side. Right-handed people have the handle on the left.

On many of the cheaper models the spools are very deep. When fishing with fine lines these spools need to be built up. This can be done by winding cotton thread on to the spool first to bring the inside of the spool nearer the rim. The nylon line is then wound on to the spool. Most tackle dealers will be willing to build the spool up.

When buying the reel, place it on your rod (by pushing the rod's reel fitting on to the reel, always at the top of the rod's handle) and see if it balances. If the outfit feels too heavy try a lighter reel.

The fixed spool reel is ideal for all forms of coarse fishing.

Line: All anglers use nylon monofilament. This comes in various sizes of breaking strains (2lb breaking strain, 6lb b.s., 12lb b.s. and so on). Again there is a wide choice of line available, both in makes and breaking strains. Whichever brand of line you choose you should always make these checks – make sure it is supple (this can be done by seeing if it falls off the spool without loops), has a small diameter and doesn't break too easily when given a sharp tug.

Having decided on the brand, what about line strength? The point to remember here is that fine lines will always catch more fish. You do not need 4lb line to make sure of landing a 3lb fish safely – with a little practice it can be done on 2lb. You may lose a big fish but it is one that probably would not have been hooked on heavier line. Surely it is better to have a shot at goal and miss than to spend all day on the pitch without ever touching the ball. The same applies to fishing. If you hook and lose a fish it gives you the incentive to go again – and you can at least talk about the one that got away.

If the reel you buy has two spools (and most have) then fill them to the rim of the spool with 2lb and 4lb line – 100 yards of each. Obviously if you are going to a spot where you know you have a very good chance of really big fish – up to 10lb – then step the heaviest line to 6lb, but that would be the absolute limit for your rod. Float rods are designed mainly for light line fishing. Fishing with really

Another popular reel – the closed faced model good for float fishing.

heavy line needs a stiffer and more powerful rod.

Hooks: These come in a variety of sizes and patterns. Sizes vary from 24's to number 1's. The higher the number the smaller the hook. They can be bought loose – either with an eye or spade end on to which you tie the line yourself – or already tied to a nylon hook length. The ready tied are obviously more expensive. They also come in forged models (which are stronger) and fine wire (weaker but sharper).

The hook is the business end of the tackle, the thing which is going to help you catch fish. The thing you must remember is that you are out to fool a fish to take a bait which has a hook in it. Therefore it stands to reason that the less chance a fish has of seeing the hook the better chance you will have of fooling it into biting.

Fine lines always catch more fish – and so do small hooks. Forget size 24's and 22's for the time being. They are specialised hooks for experienced anglers, normally match anglers (those who fish in competitions). Your aim at the start should be to carry a range of hooks which will cope with most conditions you are likely to meet on your first few outings.

My advice would be to buy 20's,

You don't need vast amounts of tackle to start with – just the basics.

18's, 16's, 14's and 12's – say ten of each, and preferably forged spade end. How to tie on spade end and eyed hooks will be dealt with later.

The key to success is to make your bait look as natural and appealing to a feeding fish as possible. The size of hooks used must be linked with the bait, the size of fish you are likely to catch and the strength of line you are using.

You wouldn't eat a piece of steak which has a big piece of metal stuck in it, so why should a fish be tempted to take your bait if the hook is showing. Therefore if you are fishing a small bait, such as single maggot, you need a small hook, that is a 20 or 18. A bigger bait such as a piece of bread can conceal a 14 or 12 hook quite easily. A single worm will not look out of place on a 16.

On the other hand, a 20 hook, hidden in a piece of bread is unsuitable because the hook is too small for the bait. The chance of hooking the fish once it has sucked in the bait are remote.

A 1lb breaking strain line would not be strong enough to strike home a 12 hook into a reasonably large fish. It's all a question of balancing your tackle.

All hooks should be tied to a line finer than the line on your reel. This enables better presentation and also if you get snagged on the bottom you will lose only your hook and not the rest of your tackle. The hook length, being finer, will break first.

Hook lengths should be about 18 inches long. Here is a guide to the strength of hook length you should use with the following hooks:

Size 20 (1lb–1½lb).
Size 18 (1½lb).
Size 16 (1½lb–2lb).
Size 14 (2lb–2½lb).
Size 12 (2½lb–4lb).

If your reel line is 2lb then 20, 18 and 16 hooks are the ones to use with the finer traces. If it is 3lb then 16 (with the heavier trace), 14 and 12 are appropriate.

Finally always make sure the hooks are needle sharp and have a fairly long shank – the length of hook between the spade-end and the bend of the hook.

Split shot and leger weights: Shot are small lead weights with splits in them. They are pinched on to the line to cock a float. If the correct amount of shot has been placed on the line only the tip of the float should show above the surface. The shot also determine the fall of the bait through the water and aid casting.

They come in various sizes but the ones you should possess are Swan, AA, BB, No's 1, 2, 4, 6, and 8. The latter is called a dust shot because it is very small. Depending on how the shot are placed on the line, the baited hook can be made to fall through the water at varying speeds *(see float fishing, chapter 7)*. Shot can be bought in

Eyed, spade and tied

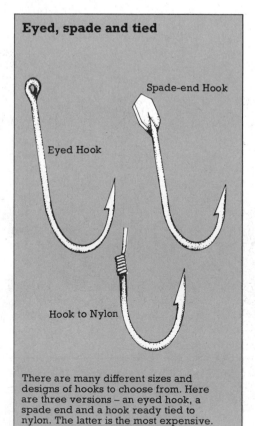

Spade-end Hook

Eyed Hook

Hook to Nylon

There are many different sizes and designs of hooks to choose from. Here are three versions – an eyed hook, a spade end and a hook ready tied to nylon. The latter is the most expensive.

dispensers but always buy the softest possible.

The most common leger weight is the arlesey bomb – a pear-shaped lead. These come in weights of ⅛oz, ¼oz, ¾oz and 1oz. The most widely used are ¼oz and ½oz. So stock up with around four of each and a couple of the heavier ones. There are also coffin leads, ball leads, barrel leads and capta leads. Coffin and capta are handy when trying to hold your bait on the bottom in fast flowing water.

Barrel and ball leads, because of their shape, allow your bait to roll along the bottom with the current. The rudiments of legering, fishing with your bait on the bottom without a float, will be explained in a later chapter.

Bank sticks and rod rests: You will need at least two bank sticks. One to screw on to a rod rest (this will support the rod when it is not being held) and one to screw on to your keepnet. When buying a screw-on rod rest, buy a wide one with a thick rubber covering so there is no chance of the line getting trapped on it.

The middle joint of your rod – if it is a three-piece rod – should be placed on the rest and the butt can be balanced

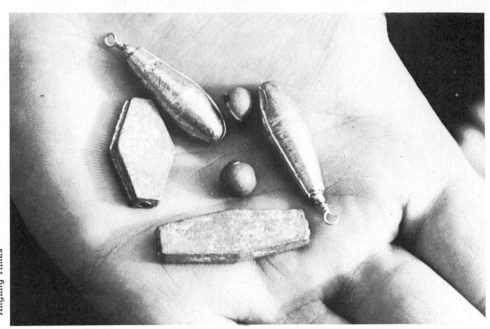

Angling Times

Three types of legers – arlesey (pear shaped), coffin and ball legers.

on the edge of your basket. If you find this awkward, then buy another rod rest and bank stick to support the butt. If you fish with the rod on the rest, make sure the tip of the rod is near the water so the wind does not interfere with the line.

Rod holdall: This is basically an

optional until you have acquired a few more rods. It is used to keep rods, umbrella, landing net pole and bank sticks in. The best models now have plastic tubes in them. Rods fit inside the tubes to protect them when being transported – but they are also fairly expensive. A home-made wide canvas bag, long enough to fit a rod and

Split shot should be kept neat and tidy, all in one box if possible.

Even the smallest fish is welcome first time out.

umbrella into, is adequate for starters.

Fishing baskets: Twenty years ago all serious anglers had wicker fishing baskets in which to carry their tackle and to sit on while fishing. Today there is a general shortage of these models. More anglers are changing to the continental wooden boxes or glass fibre versions. If you can manage to buy a good wicker basket which is closely woven for a reasonable price, snap it up. If not your father, if he is a

bit of a handy man, shouldn't find it too hard to make you a fair sized box out of plywood. Obviously it should have a lid so you can sit on it, four or six small legs to grip slopping banks. It should also have an extendable strap going through it. To start with, a haversack and a small stool will get you by.

On flowing water where you need to let your float move along with the current it is often best to stand up to achieve the best control over your

tackle.

Umbrella: A must if you intend fishing the whole year round. There is nothing worse than fishing in the rain and getting soaking wet. If you are sodden, the last thing you will want to concentrate on is catching fish. You will be forced to pack up early. The best umbrellas are those which have a tilt – the stem folds back so you can angle it in any direction that the rain is coming from rather than having to sit directly under it, which will impede casting and striking. It is also handy to protect you from cold winds.

Keepnet and landing net: The keepnet is to keep your catch in. Buy one which is 8ft long and at least 18 inches in diameter. It is unlikely you will fill even a quarter of the net on your first outings but the fish you catch must be kept in a net which is big enough for them to swim freely around without discomfort. When they are returned they will swim away none the worse for their experience. Landing nets need to be about 18 inches across. They have either round or triangular metal rims on to which the net fits. A single or extending pole is also needed on to which the net is screwed.

Floats: There are literally hundreds of different floats on the market. Anglers are great float collectors. They will buy new ranges purely because they have been recommended or because they have seen someone catch a good net of fish with a certain model. There isn't an all purpose float – you need a selection.

To fish confidently on both still and running water the following should be obtained: Waggler, stick float, balsa, antenna and slider. They all come in various sizes, each taking a different amount of shot. So buy a light, medium and heavy of each model. It is handy to

There are hundreds of floats available – a collection is built up in time.

have two of each in case one is lost. That will give you a total of 30 floats, which will meet most conditions you are likely to experience at first. As time goes on and you become proficient with each float you can search further afield for patterns which may be beneficial to certain waters you will be fishing. Floats have different coloured tips to make them clearly visible in the water. Buy floats with either red or black tops – these are the ones which stand out best.

Bits and pieces: The above are your main items of tackle but you also need some accessories. You will require a couple of plastic bait boxes in which to carry your bait, a disgorger to help free the hook from a fish which has swallowed the bait, a catapult to help fire out bait into your swim so as to attract the fish, a washing-up bowl in which to mix groundbait. A small but essential item is a plummet which is fixed on to the hook to help find the depth when float fishing *(see float fishing, chapter 7)* and last but not least a wooden box to store all these bits and pieces. It may seem a long and endless list but like any sport you need the right equipment. A golfer needs a variety of clubs to cope with all situations.

Keepnets should be as large as possible to help protect the fish.

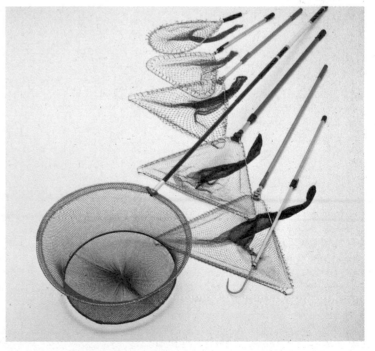

Landing nets come in various shapes. The round or triangular are good models.

CHAPTER TWO

Coarse bait - the essentials

Now you have the equipment there is still one thing left – BAIT, the item which plays the greatest part in catching fish.

Even the best tackle available is in the end dependant on the quality of bait used with it. There is no such thing as a magical formula which will always guarantee success but bait which has been carefully prepared and looked after will increase catches.

The menu anglers can prepare is seemingly endless. Exotic morsels such as cherries, sliced bananas, elderberries, peas, slugs and crayfish have all been known to catch fish. But before trying out different concoctions my advice is to master the more common ones.

A beginner should ideally catch a fish on his first outing. This will make him want to go again. So let us deal first with the most popular bait – maggots. This will catch fish of all sizes in almost any water in Britain. They are easy to obtain – all tackle dealers should stock them – and to use.

There are four main types – the commercial maggot, pinkies, squatts and gozzers. Let's start with the first one.

Commercial maggots: These are the ones produced by maggot breeders for sale over the counter. They are the result of eggs laid by the bluebottle fly. They come in a variety of colours – white (the natural colour), yellow, red and bronze (which have been dyed with Chrysodine). Thousands of gallons of maggots are used on waters throughout Britain each week. With this vast amount being thrown in regularly it has become

Maggots, casters and groundbait – enough to see you through most days.

almost a natural bait to fish.

For your first trip half a pint of mixed maggots (all the different colours together) will be quite enough. When you buy them they should be placed in a clean tin with plenty of air holes to

Hooking a maggot

Hooking a Maggot

Many people just put the hook into a maggot anyhow. Done like this the maggot will remain more active and therefore more tempting to fish, while it is in the water.

allow them to breathe and then stored in a cool place until needed. Try to buy them the day before you go fishing. In warm weather maggots will change into casters or chrysalis – the dormant state they are in before hatching into bluebottles – in three or four days. And you don't want to get to the bankside with a tin full of "turned" maggots.

When buying maggots make sure they are fresh and big. The latter is easy to spot but to ensure you are armed with fresh ones check the maggots have a black fleck under their skin. This is the food pouch which will show they have only recently been taken "off the feed". Make sure the dealer puts a handful of bran or sawdust in with your maggots – this will allow the maggots to go on cleaning themselves. Care must always be given to whatever bait you use.

If the family buys a pound of steak it is treated with respect. The meat is kept clean, fresh and cooked nicely and then served so it looks appetising. The same applies to all baits. Bait which has not been cleaned, kept in a dirty tin, has been allowed to sweat because it has not been stored in a cool place or is of an inferior quality will catch fewer fish than those which have been looked after carefully.

Pinkies: These are smaller than the commercial maggot and come from the eggs of a greenbottle fly. They are often thrown into a swim (the area you are fishing) as feeders – maggots which will help attract fish into the swim and get them feeding. They can either be thrown in loose or in ground-bait (to be dealt with later). They are softer than the bigger maggots and therefore can be more appealing to shy biting or small fish.

They are best kept in fine sawdust because they are natural escapologists if allowed to sweat or get wet. Any which have become moist and left in a container without a lid will not be there the following day. Apart from the loss of bait you will also be faced with a hatch of greenbottles a few days later.

Squatts: These are the smallest variety of maggots coming from the house fly. They are normally only used as "feeders", usually when fishing for bream. They are difficult to breed and only obtainable during the summer months. They should always be kept in red foundry sand in which they are sold as this is slightly moist and will ensure that they stay fresh for as long as possible.

Gozzers: A very specialised home-bred maggot, used mainly by match anglers when fishing for bream. The gozzer comes from a fly which will only lay its eggs on fresh meat placed out at night. The maggots to come off the fly's eggs are very soft – making them more appealing and succulent to fish.

BREEDING GOZZERS: As you become more experienced and want to branch out and experiment with various baits you may want to breed your own gozzers. It is not such a foul smelling, unsocial business as it may appear.

Buy a piece of chicken and place it in an empty tin, replacing the lid with sufficient space for the gozzer fly to crawl through. The meat should be placed out in the evening and the following morning there should be a cluster of eggs where the fly has "blown". These will hatch into gozzers.

Angling Times

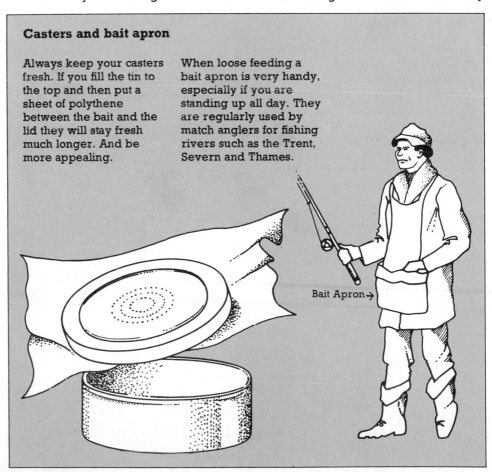

Carp, like this huge 31½lb fish prefer big baits such as bread flake.

The blown meat should be wrapped tightly in newspaper and buried in dry bran at the bottom of the tin. The meat should then be stored in a fairly warm place. In six days the gozzers should be fully grown and at a stage when they no longer want to stop on the meat and feed. They should be shaken off the meat and transferred into wet bran. This will keep them soft and take any remaining feed out of them. Gozzers can also be bred on pig's hearts or pigeon meat but this produces a darker maggot.

Casters: This is the second most popular bait to maggots. A caster is a maggot which is beginning to turn into a chrysalis. It should be a light golden brown and sink when thrown into the water. Many anglers buy their maggots in bulk and get their own casters by

Casters and bait apron

Always keep your casters fresh. If you fill the tin to the top and then put a sheet of polythene between the bait and the lid they will stay fresh much longer. And be more appealing.

When loose feeding a bait apron is very handy, especially if you are standing up all day. They are regularly used by match anglers for fishing rivers such as the Trent, Severn and Thames.

Bait Apron →

Hooking a caster

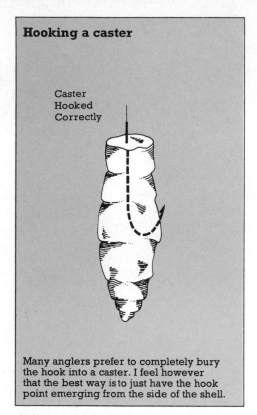

Caster Hooked Correctly

Many anglers prefer to completely bury the hook into a caster. I feel however that the best way is to just have the hook point emerging from the side of the shell.

leaving the maggots to start "turning" and then put them through a fine mesh riddle. The casters will stay on the top while the maggots wriggle through, but this is a time-consuming task. Tackle dealers sell casters. They are more expensive than maggots because of the work involved. Stay clear of casters which are sold in pre-sealed packs as the plastic bags tend to mark the casters' skin and you never know exactly how long they have been kept.

Again you should ask for the freshest bait the dealer has. Most dealers run their casters off every day to keep a supply of fresh bait. After you have

bought your casters it is best to put them all in a bucket of water, skim off any which float and then sieve the rest free of water. Place the casters in a clean container, pack them as tight as possible and put a thin sheet of polythene between the lid and the box to make the container airtight. They should be used shortly afterwards or else they will go sour and put fish off the feed rather than making them accept the bait.

Worms: Worms have been used since time immemorial and like maggots will tempt most freshwater fish. There are three main varieties – brandlings, redworms and lobworms.

Brandlings are the ones which have the small yellow rings at intervals along their body while redworms are smaller and redder. They are much more lively when on the hook and, like brandlings, can be found in most manure or compost heaps. I recommend you to find your own supply of worms as tackle dealers tend to charge quite a lot for even the smallest tub of worms. Once you've found your worms keep them in a tin with plenty of damp compost or moss.

Lobworms are rarely sold in shops but can be dug in the garden or picked from lawns during early morning or after a spell of wet weather. They can also be found coming out from between paving slabs after a rainfall. Keep them in a tin together with a mixture of moss, earth and grass.

If you take worms with you always have at least 50 in your box when using brandlings or redworms. A couple of dozen lobworms per outing will normally see you through.

Worm as bait

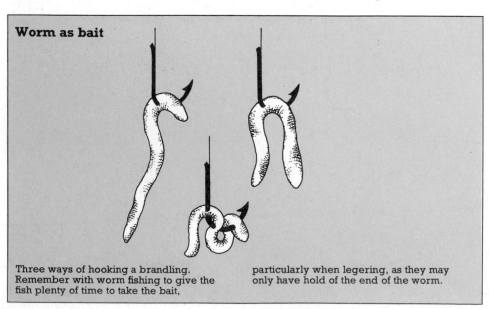

Three ways of hooking a brandling. Remember with worm fishing to give the fish plenty of time to take the bait, particularly when legering, as they may only have hold of the end of the worm.

Use your loaf

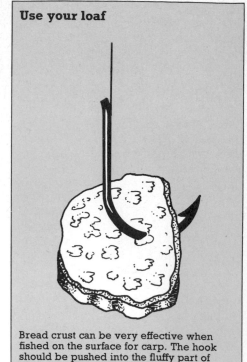

Bread crust can be very effective when fished on the surface for carp. The hook should be pushed into the fluffy part of the bread and pulled through the crust. This will ensure it stays on the hook.

Bread: Another inexpensive bait which can be used in several forms – flake, paste, crust or with a bread punch (a small metal gadget which punches out small round flakes from a sliced loaf). Flake should be taken from a fresh loaf – I prefer thin sliced – and the size of the flake depends very much on the size of fish you hope to catch.

Paste can be made from either fresh or stale bread. Remove the crusts, put it it in a bowl, soak in water and mix it with your hands. If it goes too soggy add more bread until it starts to stiffen up. You will have reached the right texture when the mixture no longer clings to your hands. Keep in a damp cloth until you need to use it.

The crust from a loaf can be used on the hook. Normally it is free-lined, placed on a hook tied to the reel line without any lead weights attached. This rig is cast out and the crust allowed to float about on the surface, normally when fishing for surface feeding carp.

Bread punches are great aids for canal fishing. Different sizes of shop bought "punches" are used, depending on the size of the hook employed. A slice of bread should be placed on a hard surface, the point of the punch pushed into it and the small piece of bread lodged in the punch transferred to the hook so that the tip of the hook is just showing. Again, the bread should be as fresh as possible.

Bread punches come in many shapes and forms. The best is the barrel type which has different sized attachments. Excellent for canal fishing.

Hemp, tares and wheat: These are collectively known as cereal baits. These all have to be cooked before they are any good to use. Some dealers do sell these baits pre-packed but a better quality can be prepared if you buy the seeds raw. Hemp is a small dark seed which should be placed in a pan of boiling water and simmered until the white kernel is showing. Sieve off the water and place the seeds in a bait tin. They are very good as loose feed (throwing them in the swim you are fishing) in conjunction with maggots or casters as a hook bait.

Tare: These are pigeon peas. They should be placed in a pan together with a heaped teaspoon of bicarbonate of soda. Pour boiling water until the pan is full and leave overnight. The following morning they should be boiled in the water they have been standing in and then simmered for about 15 minutes. After this time they should be checked to see if they are soft enough to squeeze.

As soon as they are, tip them into a sieve and place them under the hot water tap and rinse them thoroughly. With hemp as loose feed they are an excellent bait on the hook when fishing for roach.

Wheat should be prepared on the same lines as hemp but an easy way is to place them in a thermos flask of boiling water, screw on the top and leave overnight. In the morning they will be well stewed and ready for use on the hook.

Luncheon meat: Choose the tinned variety with a high meat content. Meat should never be cut into cubes. It should be cut into $\frac{1}{4}$ to $\frac{1}{2}$ inch slices and then pieces broken off to size. The hook should be gently pushed into the meat and around any gristle which may be in it. The cast should be smooth without any sudden jerks which might make the meat fall off.

Cheese: Whichever you use, the cheese must be soft enough to allow the hook to pull through on the strike.

Wired up

Hemp Fishing

Lead Wire

When fishing with hemp seed false bites can occur because the feeding fish mistake split shot on the line for the bait. The problem can be overcome by putting a small piece of coiled wire onto the line (above) or a mouse dropping lead.

Bread flake

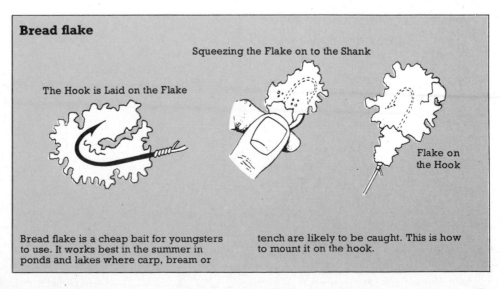

Squeezing the Flake on to the Shank

The Hook is Laid on the Flake

Flake on the Hook

Bread flake is a cheap bait for youngsters to use. It works best in the summer in ponds and lakes where carp, bream or tench are likely to be caught. This is how to mount it on the hook.

If it is still on after striking, then it is too hard. It's a very good bait for chub and I have also landed carp and roach on it. I prefer to use the pre-packed sliced variety. This is soft enough to be used straight from the pack.

Sweetcorn: A bait which has been highly successful in the past few years for carp and tench. There is no preparation involved – use it straight from the tin. But remember always to take used tins home with you – don't leave them on the bank.

Groundbait: This normally consists of bread crumbs mixed with water. Just enough water should be added so that the groundbait can be made into a soft, fluffy mix. It is not used on the hook but thrown in the swim as an attractor of fish. It can be used on its own but is most effective when baits such as pinkies, squatts or casters are added. These can be placed into the swim more accurately and sent further than loose feeding.

The groundbait should be mixed in a fairly large bowl and the water stirred well into the crumbs to ensure a thorough mix. If it is too wet the mix will be difficult to throw out without breaking up in mid-air. Too little water and the mix will be too hard. Your aim should be to get the mix just right. In stillwater – where there is little or no flow – the mix containing plenty of loose feed, should break up on the surface. In faster moving water, mix it a little more stiffly so that the ball breaks up on the way to the bottom of the river bed.

Groundbait can be the secret of a good day's fishing if done correctly. It must be placed into the swim correctly and in a small area. It's no good scattering it everywhere – that will just split up the fish which are in your swim. The idea is to concentrate the groundbait into a small area – where you can cast your tackle comfortably. Remember it is no good getting the fish feeding in a spot you cannot cast to. So first cast out to a comfortable mark; then throw your groundbait in the area.

With groundbait, remember the motto "Little and often". Too much groundbait all at once can frighten the fish or fill them up too quickly. If you were hungry and given a whole loaf in one go you would be able to eat so much but have to leave the rest . . . if you were given a slice every now and again during the day you could eat

much more. The same applies to fish.

When mixing groundbait, never mix the whole bag all at once. If you don't use it all it cannot be saved but if you only mix small amount at a time there will always be some in reserve. Then you can always mix a bit more if need be.

All the above baits have been prepared as a list for you to follow. Please don't think you have to carry all of them with you on your first visit. My aim has been to make you familiar with some of the popular baits available so that you will recognise them when they are mentioned later in the book.

When you make your first fishing trip my advice would be to take half a pint of mixed maggots, some worms, a couple of slices of bread and a small bag of groundbait. The three baits will give you plenty of permutations and you will also be able to practice the art of mixing the groundbait, adding the maggots to it and groundbaiting the swim accurately.

Too many baits will cause confusion to the beginner. Make yourself at home with maggots, worms and bread and then you can spread your wings further and experiment with all the others.

The exact use of many of the above

baits will be described in more detail later in the book.

Now let's have a look at the freshwater fish you are likely to catch and the baits which will attract them.

Cocktails

Worm Maggot Cocktail

A cocktail bait can sometimes be a killer for bream. The most common is a worm placed on the hook just through the middle and then the hook is tipped with a single maggot.

Mix groundbait nice and fluffy and as soft as possible when fishing on stillwater. Always add a few hookbait samples such as maggots or casters.

Big perch have been rare in recent years but with a bit of careful scouting, lakes and rivers containing fish of this size can still be found. Favourite baits are lobworm, redworm or maggots.

CHAPTER THREE

Know your coarse fish

Before setting off to the bank, let's have a look at some of Britain's most popular coarse fish, where you can catch them, their habits and the baits used to land them. It is enjoyable to catch your first fish but some of the excitement can be lost if you don't know exactly what you have hooked. The following is a list of the main coarse fish you are likely to meet.

BARBEL *(Barbus barbus)*
Record, 13lb 12oz

Identification: The barbel is a muscular streamlined fish, built for speed in fast moving water. The back of its rounded tapering body is a dark olive-green, the sides a paler shade of green/brown and the belly is cream or white. It has a thick-lipped mouth. It has four barbels attached to its mouth – two at the front of the upper lip and one at each corner. Its dorsal fin (the one on its back) is fairly short and the tail is deeply forked, having two differently shaped lobes – the upper one being pointed and the lower rounded.

Location: Barbel prefer swift, clean, moving water with a gravel bottom. That is why they are not spread across all of Britain. Main barbel rivers used to be the Hants Avon, Dorset Stour, the Thames, the Kennet, and Yorkshire rivers such as the Ouse, Swale and Ure. Now, however, they are well estab-

Pike can be exciting fish to catch no matter what size.

lished in the mighty River Severn and the barbel population of the River Trent is increasing each season.

Feeding habits and baits: As the positioning of its mouth may suggest, the barbel feeds on the bottom, grubbing around for whatever it can find. Maggots, casters, luncheon meat, cheese, worms and bread – in fact, all the baits I mentioned earlier – will tempt this fish provided the bait is fished on or near the bottom. Fish of just a couple of pounds put up a tremendous fight so fairly hefty tackle is needed. Barbel feed best during the warmer months.

BLEAK *(Alburnus alburnus)*
Record, 3oz 15 drams.

Identification: Looks like a tiny herring. This silvery fish has an olive to grey-green back and silver sides and belly. Its fins are very pale. They have an upturned mouth and rarely exceed six inches in length.

Location: Mainly found in slow-moving rivers of the South, especially the Thames, East and Midlands.

Feeding habits and baits: Its upturned mouth shows that it feeds mainly on or just below the surface. In the

summer can be found in huge shoals and will boil on the surface when a handful of maggots or casters are thrown in. A good fish for beginners to practice on because they are easy to catch. Best bait is single maggot on a size 18's or 20's hook.

BREAM *(Abramis brama)*
Record, 13lb 8oz.

Identification: Very deep fish with a pronounced hump on its back. The fully grown fish has a dark greeny-brown or bronze back but when young tends to be silver. Has a thick-lipped mouth which can extend down to enable it to feed on the bottom. Its body is covered in a thick protective slime.

Location: A shoal fish widespread in England and Ireland. Most common in lakes or slow-moving rivers and Fenland drains.

Feeding habits and baits: Predominantly bottom feeders. If you catch one your chances of catching more are greatly increased, for the whole shoal usually feeds at the same time. Will accept a variety of baits, including maggots, casters, worms, bread in all its forms and sweetcorn.

COMMON CARP (Cyprinus carpio)
Record, 44lb.

Identification: Has a thickset and deep bronze to golden body. The dorsal fin is long and concave and its mouth has four barbels on it – two on each side. There are two other forms of carp very similar to the common – mirror and leather carp. The mirror has only a few big scales across its back while the leather has no scales.

Location: Found throughout Britain mainly in lakes and ponds. Canals or rivers where warm water flows in from power stations are good spots for carp as they thrive well in warm water. The River Trent now has a good head of carp. Fished for mainly during the summer months.

Feeding habits and baits: Feed either on the surface or the bottom. Serious carp anglers mix their own concoctions of high protein baits to land the 20lb plus fish but carp can be caught on floating crust, paste or flake, sweetcorn, worms, cheese, maggots and casters. Hemp seed is a good attractor.

CRUCIAN CARP (Carassius carassius)
Record, 5lb 10½oz.

Identification: Much smaller than the common carp. Has no barbels, a very rounded body and is a bronze-reddish colour.

Location: Widespread in England but normally only found in lakes and ponds. A few canals contain them.

Feeding habits and baits: Normally only caught on or near the bottom. Fish of only a few ounces can put up a great tussle on light tackle. Baits are the same as for common carp.

CHUB (Lauciscus cephalus)
Record, 7lb 6oz.

Identification: Has a grey-green back with big silvery-yellow scales on its sides. Its fins have a reddish tinge and its mouth – very big for its size – has large thick lips on it. Its dorsal fin is convex.

Location: Chub prefer fast-flowing water and can be found in streams and rivers throughout England, except Cornwall. Can often be found in shoals, especially in the shallower runs in summer or in spots surrounded by overhanging trees or margin weed.

Feeding habits and baits: Chub will feed all the year round, even in the coldest conditions. All the baits mentioned previously will catch them and

A small bream – a common fish on lakes and rivers in summer.

even more exotic morsels such as slugs, wasp grub and minnows will tempt them.

DACE (Leuciscus leuciscus)
Record, 1lb 4¼oz.

Identification: Not to be confused with small chub or bleak. Has a dark olive back with silvery sides. Its dorsal fin is concave. Its fins are pale, sometimes with a pink tinge. Has a fairly small rubbery mouth.

Location: Found in the same type of waters as chub, throughout England except Cornwall.

Feeding habits and baits: Dace are shoal fish but at times can be very finicky and will produce fast bites. Can be caught at all depths of water in most conditions. Maggots, casters, bread and worms are the most effective baits fished with float tackle.

EEL (Anguilla anguilla)
Record 11lb 2oz.

Identification: Its snake-like features make it easy to identify. Its dorsal fin starts a little way back from its head and extends all the way to its tail. It is either a yellow or silver colour. Only silver when it is making its way to the sea to swim across the Atlantic,

eventually to spawn in the Sargasso Sea.

Location: Common throughout Britain. Found in rivers, streams and some land-locked waters.

Feeding habits and baits: Eels will eat anything they find on the bottom. Feed best in the evening and during the warmer months. Can be a nuisance when trying to catch other bottom-feeding fish but when hooked will give a very good account of themselves.

GUDGEON (Gobio gobio)
Record, 4¼oz.

Identification: Its colouring changes a lot depending where it is caught. Some have a silvery body; others bronze to almost black. Has a downturned mouth with two barbels projecting from the corners. Can resemble baby barbel.

Location: Very common in rivers, streams and canals in England except Cornwall. Prefer the deeper slow-moving parts of a water.

Feeding habits and baits: Bottom feeders, usually found in shoals. Can be good fun for beginners to catch. Fish with light tackle on the bottom with maggot as hook bait.

Continued on page 22

Rudd

Common Carp

Gudgeon

Perch

Common Bream

Roach

Pike

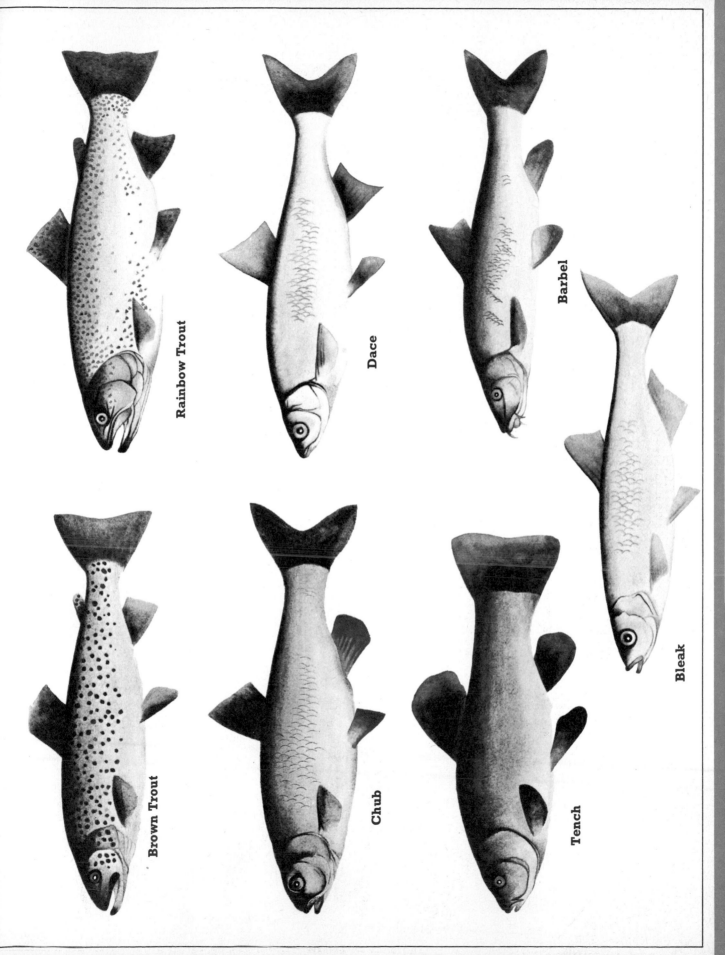

Rainbow Trout

Dace

Barbel

Brown Trout

Chub

Tench

Bleak

PERCH (*Perca fluviatilis*)
Record, 4lb 12oz.

Identification: Easily distinguished by its black strips on its olive-green back and sides. Has a spiney dorsal fin and its lower fins are a dull red. Has a large mouth.

Location: Not as common as they once were. Most waters in Britain still hold perch but not in the same quantity as 20 years ago. Canals and lakes are still the best areas to find them in numbers.

Feeding habits and baits: Many top anglers will tell you their first fish was a perch. Best bait is a small worm or a couple of maggots fished near the bottom. When the perch takes the bait it will often swallow it. In these circumstances it is often better to cut the hook length if you cannot see the hook rather than damage the fish by proding around with a disgorger.

PIKE (*Esox lucius*)
Record, 40lb.

Identification: The colouring of its body is a mottled green and yellow, darker on its back than its sides. It has a long tapering body, the head is large and its mouth, very much like a wide duck's bill, is full of needle sharp teeth.

Location: Found everywhere in Britain. The bigger the water, the larger pike tend to grow.

Feeding habits and baits: Pike are predators, feeding on smaller fish such as dace, roach and rudd. Waters with plenty of weed cover are ideal for pike as these fish like to lie in cover waiting for their prey. Can be caught on spinners, worms, dead or live fish. Feed best in winter.

ROACH (*Rutilus rutilus*)
Record, 4lb 1oz.

Identification: A lovely coloured fish. Has a dark grey back, silver sides and red fins. The mouth is fairly small with a projecting upper lip.

Location: Found in most waters in Britain. Probably the most popular species because they are so common. In fastish flowing water fish of 6oz can really make your rod bend. Can be caught at all depths but mainly on or near the bottom. All the baits mentioned will catch roach but most common are maggots, casters, hemp and bread.

RUDD (*Scardinius erythrophthalmus*)
Record, 4lb 8oz.

Identification: Similar to a roach but is a more golden colour and its fins are a brighter red. Its mouth has an up-turned bottom lip to enable it to feed near the surface.

Location: Widespread in England, Wales and Ireland. They prefer still waters such as ponds, lakes, Fenland drains and canals but can sometimes be caught in slow-moving rivers.

Feeding habits and bait: Mainly a summer fish which feeds on or near the surface. Rudd can be seen rising freely on hot summer evenings when flies are hatching. Small baits such as maggots, casters and pinches of bread flake, float-fished near the surface or on the drop (with the bait falling slowly through the water) will catch them.

RUFFE (*Acerina cernua*)
Record, 5oz.

Identification: A member of the perch family but much smaller in size. Has brownish body covered with darker spots, a small spiney dorsal fin and has gill covers with sharp edges.

Location: Known in the South as Pope. Also common in the Eastern and Midlands rivers and drains.

Feeding habits and baits: Ruffe feed on the bottom and will accept maggots, casters and small worms. Not a very exciting fish to catch for they put up little resistance when hooked.

TENCH (*Tinca tinca*)
Record, 10lb 1oz 2 drams.

Identification: A marvellous hard-fighting fish, which has a dark olive colour with a yellow belly. A thick-set fish, with rounded fins, it is quite slim. Its scales are very tiny, giving it a smooth skin, and its eyes are red.

Location: Found in ponds, lakes and canals throughout Britain, except Northern Scotland. Most slow-moving rivers also hold a few tench, normally found where there is the greatest weed cover.

Feeding habits and baits: Tench feed best during the summer with early morning and late evening being the best times. They grub around the bottom, in areas near weed-beds. When a shoal of tench are feeding, small pin-head sized bubbles will appear in your swim as they stir up the bottom. Sweetcorn, bread, worms, maggots and casters are the most common baits.

TROUT: The two main types of trout found in British waters are Brown and Rainbow.

BROWN TROUT (*Salmo trutta*)
Record, 19lb 9¼oz)

Identification: As its name suggests it is basically brown in colouring.

Not a large catch of bream and perch but one which would delight most beginners. Fish of this size are more fun to catch on light tackle.

While its back may be a very dark to golden brown and brown trouts stomach is normally a creamy white. It is easily identifiable by the large red spots found along its back and flanks. The spots do however vary in colour (sometimes a light brown) and size depending on its environment. Being a member of the salmon family the brown trout has the tell tale adipose fin (a small gristley fin) placed near its tail.

Location: Found in streams, lakes and rivers throughout Britain. Brown trout in streams and rivers tend to be "wild" fish which have lived all their life in the same water. While some of them do reach a weight of as much as 6lb the most common size is around 4oz to 1lb. Bigger wild fish can be found in Scotland's and Ireland's vast lakes and these can reach record breaking sizes. Chalk streams, normally strictly private, also had very large fish. Nowadays brown trout are found in most of Britain's fly fishing reservoirs and lakes where they are stocked by the owners of the water. They are usually placed into the fishery at around 1lb after being reared in small ponds, by commercial fish breeders. At some waters such as Rutland and Grafham fish of 4lb plus are regularly caught but a 2lb brownie is still regarded as an excellent fish.

Feeding habits and bait: Brown trout will eat almost anything from bread, maggots and worms to grasshoppers and caterpillars but most fisheries which contain trout have strict rules – they may only be fished for with artificial flies (explained later). By using lines which either sink or float the artificial fly can be presented either on the bottom or on the surface (wet and dry fly fishing). In cold weather brown trout tend to stay near the bottom grubbing around in the mud while during the warmer months can be seen rising on the surface snapping up insects which are either hatching or landing on the water.

RAINBOW TROUT *(Salmo gairdneri)*
Record, 19lb 8oz)

Identification: Has the same sort of streamlined shaped as a brown trout but its colouring is much more vivid. Some rainbow trout can be almost completely silver while others will have a definite pinkish streak running along their flanks. When hooked the rainbow trout is more likely to leap out of the water several times during the fight in a bid to shead the hook.

Location: Unlike brown trout there are very few waters in Britain where the rainbow breeds naturally. They are very popular in the ever increasing still water fisheries because they are usually easier to catch than brown trout prefering to feed on or near the surface in most conditions. They are also a hit with fish farmers who breed trout for use as stock fish because rainbows have a much faster growing rate than browns. They are normally placed into waters at around 1lb although some fisheries have now adopted a policy of stocking with fish between 3lb and 15lb to attract more anglers to their water. They are most common in Midland, and Southern waters although some lakes in Scotland and Wales are now stocked.

Feeding habits and baits: If a trout water does allow bait fishing then worms or a small spinner can be very effective when after rainbow trout but you will find that nearly all fisheries again apply the fly only rule. When rainbow trout are really feeding – and they normally swim round in small shoals – they will take any pattern of fly cast to them. At times like this it is not uncommon to catch four or five fish in a matter of minutes before the shoal moves on. While brown trout tend to feed best at dawn and dusk the beauty with rainbows is that there are usually always odd fish feeding throughout the day – even in the worst conditions.

ZANDER *(Stizostedion lucioperca)*
Record, 17lb 4oz.

Identification: Sometimes known as a pike-perch but it is not a hybrid (a cross between the two fishes). Zander have a long tapering body, a dark green back and paler sides with broad vertical stripes but not as pronounced as that of the perch. It has a large mouth, with sharp teeth and a spiney dorsal.

Location: These fish were imported from the continent and placed in the Great Ouse, Norfolk. They have now spread through other fenland waters. Also found in a few lakes in the South.

Feeding habits and baits: The zander is not much liked. It is a predator and feeds in packs – always on small fish. They have been blamed for the decline in other coarse fish in the fens. Can be caught on spinners or bunches of worms but the best methods are either live-baiting or dead-baiting with small rudd or roach.

This 7lb 3oz specimen eel took some holding. The biggest eels come from lakes.

CHAPTER FOUR

How to catch your first fish

For your first fishing trip, I would recommend you to find a water such as a small lake or pond, which is teeming with small roach, rudd and carp. While many of them are private or club waters, others are open to anglers on a day ticket permit – usually very reasonably priced.

If such a water doesn't exist in your area, then go to your local canal or river – but pick a stretch where the water moves slowly – this will make life much easier when learning the rudiments. Most rivers hold a quantity of small fish and these will be the ones you will practise on.

Once at the water's edge you will need to assemble your tackle correctly. Here are the basics to tackling up:

The rod: Push the top joint into the middle joint and then these two sections into the butt joint, making sure the eyes on the rod all line up.

The reel: Push the reel on to the rod's reel fittings, making sure it is firmly secure at the top of the handle. Now open the metal bail arm on the reel and thread the line through ALL of the rings one by one, starting with the butt ring and finishing with the end eye. Pull the line down level with your handle and then engage the bail

Always look for a "fishy" spot when setting up. Overhanging trees or weed beds are natural "homes" for most coarse fish.

arm by turning the handle of the reel. This will click it over.

Attaching the float: On any still water you will be using a float which is attached by the bottom only. These are wagglers and antennas. The small wire ring at the bottom of these floats

After casting the tackle out the rod should either be held or placed in a rod rest close to hand.

should be threaded on to the line and then locked with two split shot (to be dealt with in a minute).

Hooks: You need a finer line on which to attach the hook to your reel line. As I have said, the hook length should be slightly lighter than the reel line. If you have tackled up with 2lb line, make sure you have a spool of 1.7lb line in your box. Take off about 18 inches, make a small loop in one end and tie this end to your reel line. Use a blood knot *(as shown)* to tie it on. On the end of your hook length comes the hook. This will be either an eyed or spade end. Remember if you have bought hooks attached to nylon, you will not need a hook length as this is already provided with these models. Just tie the hook to nylon straight on to your reel line.

An eyed hook is also tied with a blood knot but the spade end types are a little more tricky. With a little practice at home you can easily master this before making your first cast. *(The diagram on page 28 explains clearly how the hook should be tied. Remember always to keep the hook length tight when tying a hook on.)* Use the line guide already mentioned to select your hook size.

Get the right curve

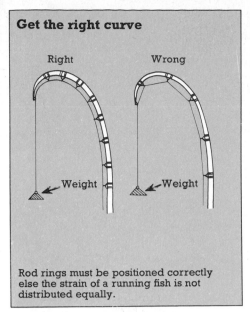

Right   Wrong

← Weight   ← Weight

Rod rings must be positioned correctly else the strain of a running fish is not distributed equally.

Shotting: Shotting is a vital aspect of float fishing. Many anglers have their floats shotted incorrectly – either they have too much float showing or the way they place their shot on the line is wrong. There are three reasons for putting shot on the line – to make the bait fall through the water naturally; to give you the weight required to cast out; and to cock the float (make it sit upright in the water) so there is little resistance for the fish to feel when taking the bait. I have already mentioned the different sized shot you will need. Today many floats you buy have their shotting capacity on them. If a float's shotting capacity is two swan shot it would be impracticable

Blood knot

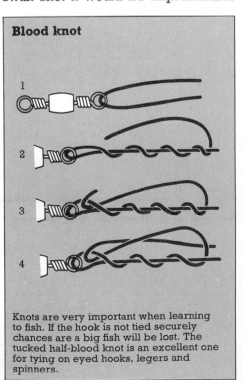

1

2

3

4

Knots are very important when learning to fish. If the hook is not tied securely chances are a big fish will be lost. The tucked half-blood knot is an excellent one for tying on eyed hooks, legers and spinners.

to put two of these shot – the biggest available – on the line and cast out. The approach is to break down the shot to the required amount, using many of the different sizes available. The bulk of the shot should be around the float. This will make casting easier. The rest of the shot should be placed on the line so the bait falls slowly through the water and also cuts out tangles when casting.

Example: If the float you have placed on your line takes two swan then a swan and an AA should be used to lock the float (set the float at about five feet and pinch the swan above the float, push the float tight up against the swan and then pinch on the AA. Now the float cannot move up and down the line). Two AA equals one swan, so it stands to reason one more AA will cock the float. This AA can be broken down even further. Two BB = one AA and two No 4's = one BB.

Whatever depth you are fishing, place the BB and No 4 just below half way between the float and the hook

and then a further No 4 between the two shot and the hook. The BB and No 4 should always be as close together as possible. You then have a total of five shot on the line – a swan, an AA, a BB and two No 4's two swan. After casting out the float will cock up, cock still further down as the BB and No 4 reach their limit and the final No 4 will submerge the float to the correct level.

The float should always be cocked so that only the tip is visible on the surface. If a two swan float doesn't cock after putting these shot on the line – and sometimes the markings given on manufactured floats are slightly out – just add another small shot to the BB and No 4 until the float sits correctly.

Plumbing the depth: A most important procedure and one which should never be neglected. On any water you will want to know how deep your swim is. By placing a plummet on to the hook (pushing the hook through the wire loop and into the cork strip) cast out at your set depth –

Bream of this size are easier to catch with leger tackle.

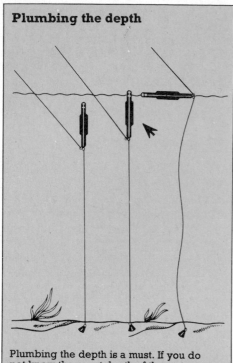

Plumbing the depth is a must. If you do not know the exact depth of the water you can spend all day fishing "blind". Depth finding is simple – just fix a plummet onto your hook and move the float about until it just shows.

say five feet. If the float disappears the swim is deeper than five feet and the float and locking shot have to be moved up the line. If the float just cocks as it should, the swim is shallower and the float and shot have to be moved down.

It is easier to plumb the depth when only the locking shot has been pinched on. When you have found the depth then add the other shot at the correct intervals. (See plumbing diagram.)

Baiting up: Your tackle should now be set correctly with the hook just on or near the bottom. To start with, maggots are as good a bait as any. With a size 20 hook use just a single maggot and with 18 or 16, a double maggot. The point of the hook should be pushed very gently into the maggot's skin, making sure not to burst the maggot. When placed on the hook (as shown on page 12) the maggot will remain lively and tempting.

Casting: This can be a tricky operation for beginners but it really is just a question of timing and positioning the rod at the correct angle. Casting can be better explained with a series of pictures (*see page 29*).

Bites: There are three main ways a fish takes the bait on float tackle – taking the float down, lifting it up, or running with it. A fish which moves

off with the bait after the tackle has reached the bottom will take the float under (unless you have the last shot on the bottom and it will then signal a lift bite as the weight is lifted from its resting place). A lift bite is normally registered when a fish intercepts the bait as it is falling through the water. This can be seen as the tackle is beginning to settle. The float will cock – but the tip will stand out of the water higher than normally because the No 4 shot you have near the hook has not reached its limit. A fish holds it up as it swims away with the bait.

Runs are more common on still waters where fish will at times move slowly along the bottom after picking up the bait.

When casting, the action should be a gentle, smooth one. If conditions allow it, it is always better to sit down and cast on narrow waterways as it causes less bankside disturbance.

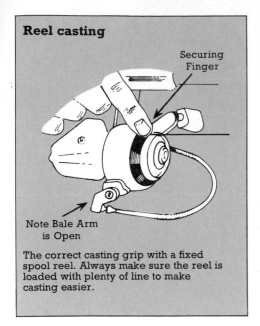
Striking: It is not enough just to get a bite to enable you to catch a fish – you have to be able to strike at the bites – that is, to lift the rod sharply up to set the hook into the fish's mouth. The strike should always be smooth, carried out with the whole length of your forearm. The handle of the rod should stay as close as possible to your arm. Do not strike with your wrist.

Your strike should be hard enough to set the hook home – but not too hard or else you could easily snap the line if a big fish has picked up the bait. In deepish water – anything over four feet – the strike should be an upward movement. In shallow water of only a couple of feet, strike to the side. This will stop the tackle tangling if you miss a bite. Strike upwards in shallow water and if you miss the bite the float and hook will fly out of the water and it is odds-on that the line will ravel up.

Playing a fish: Small fish should be wound in carefully and swung in to the hand. Try to judge the distance between the rod top and the fish and then swing the fish in so that it comes to your hand. Too much line out and the fish will still be in the water as you lift the tackle out. Too little line and the fish will end up half way up the rod – forcing you to let out more line by back-winding. Many youngsters swing the fish on to the bank and then put the rod down and walk to the fish. This is wrong. You should always be aiming to make things as easy as possible. If you happen to hook into a big fish, take your time. Allow the rod to bend but if the fish starts to swim off quickly

Place the reel at the top of the rod butt and you cannot go far wrong. You then have complete control.

Use the forearm, placed along the rod butt, to play a big fish. This will help put the correct amount of pressure on the fish.

Angling Times

give it some line by back-winding. (Winding the reel the opposite way without the ratchet on. It is always best to fish with the ratchet off.) The rod should always have a slight bend in it when playing a large fish – never allow the line to go slack. As the fish starts to tire, keep its head out of the water as it reaches the surface but be ready for the fish to make sudden dives and again give out line. Once the fish is completely exhausted place the landing net under it and scoop it out (*see diagram*).

Unhooking: All fish should be unhooked carefully and gently. If the hook is in a fish's lips take hold of the hook's shank and pull the point out gently. A disgorger should be used on a fish which has swallowed the bait – use a disgorger with a small slit in the side. This slit is placed on the hook-length, making sure the line is tight. Slide it down into the fish's mouth to be pushed gently against the hook. This should force it out. If you cannot get the hook out don't keep prodding about, cut the line as near to the hook as possible and quickly put the fish in the keepnet or return it to the water. No fish should be kept out of water for more than a few seconds.

Here are some important points to remember. Some of them will be dealt with in greater detail in the float-

. Always shot the float up carefully.
. Plumb the depth correctly and fish near the bottom.
. Always throw in a few maggots – or whatever hookbait you are using – around the float. Say six to a dozen maggots or casters every five minutes and continue to feed when the fish start biting. Small, soft balls of groundbait as described earlier can be thrown in but not quite so often as with loose feed. Always place loose feed into your groundbait.
. Change your hookbait after catching a fish.
. With mixed maggots you get different colours. If, say, white hasn't caught any fish then change to red or yellow or a combination of the colours.

Tying a spade-end

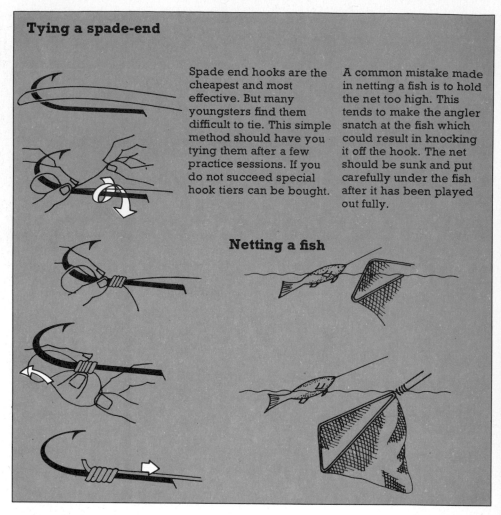

Spade end hooks are the cheapest and most effective. But many youngsters find them difficult to tie. This simple method should have you tying them after a few practice sessions. If you do not succeed special hook tiers can be bought.

A common mistake made in netting a fish is to hold the net too high. This tends to make the angler snatch at the fish which could result in knocking it off the hook. The net should be sunk and put carefully under the fish after it has been played out fully.

Netting a fish

fishing chapter.

Your fishing techniques will be very much improved if you are lucky enough to have an experienced angler with you on the banks to show you the ropes. Many areas have angling clubs with thriving junior section, which also organise tutorial classes. If there is one in your area, my advice is to join. Reading about the basics and then being shown them in practice is the quickest way to learn.

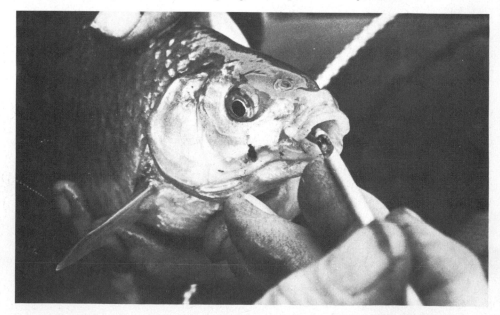

Fish should be unhooked very carefully. If the hook has been swallowed always use a disgorger.

The first essential when casting either with float or leger tackle is to hold the rod correctly. If you are right handed the left hand should be holding the butt right at the bottom. To give complete control the line should be trapped by the finger on the edge of the spool.

With the correct grip bring the rod back to the angle shown. To cast forward the left hand should pull down on the bottom of the butt causing the rod to pivot on the extended right arm. As the rod comes forward release the line. The finger which trapped the line in the first place should then be used to "feather" (lightly touch the spool as the tackle flies through the air) the tackle onto the water.

Body and rod should always be lined up square on the target area. With floats such as wagglers (which are attached bottom only) and when leger fishing always pass the tackle straight over your head for greatest accuracy. The procedure may seem complicated at first but once the timing of the cast has been perfected you will be able to hit the required area every time.

CHAPTER FIVE

Habitats of coarse fish

Going fishing, most anglers get cracking on the nearest swim. But that's like someone going into a field blindfold, aiming a shot gun into the air and hoping to shoot a pheasant. A fish is a wild animal and must be stalked in the same way as game.

A cut off from the main river can provide super sport especially when the main river is in flood. The off-shoot will provide shelter.

The old saying that time spent in reconnaisance is never wasted is worth remembering. No water has fish distributed equally along the whole fishery. Fish are creatures of habit, especially the larger ones, and have their own territory. While some swims may be ideal for anglers, having no snags in the water, easy access and a comfortable bank on which to place your basket, it may not be the most appealing to fish.

So spend as much time as possible studying the water and thinking to yourself "Where would I swim if I were a fish?" Likely areas often stand out.

A lake or pond will have most fish where the weed growth is at its highest. So fish on the edge of weedbeds, rather than in completely weed-free water. All fish especially tench, carp and rudd, prefer to swim around weed beds, which are natural feeding grounds, looking for food.

The same applies to streams, canals and rivers. In the summer months margin weed will be clearly visible. Fish just past this weed cover and your chances will be greatly increased. Overhanging trees and bushes are also likely places for these can provide shelter and food for fish such as roach, chub and dace. They will hide under the branches and feed on insects falling off them.

By plumbing the depth you can get a good picture of the bottom of any fishery. It may be that the water you will fish has a fairly uniform depth but usually the depth varies a great deal, especially in gravel pits and the larger rivers.

During the summer it is best to fish in the shallower reaches. On rivers and streams fish will congregate in the shallower water because it provides more oxygen for them. In stillwater the shallows are warmer than the deeper areas.

In winter, however, the reverse is true. Fish drop back into the deep runs and go down to the bottom where the water is at its warmest, so look for the deeper swims.

Fishing flooded rivers also calls for a keen eye. Swims which produce fish in normal conditions may be useless once the river's level has risen. The swims may be too fast or turbulent for fish to stay there. In these conditions they will drop into any slack pieces of water. Slacks can be found where the bank cuts away, forming a small bay. Cattle drinking places can be very good holding areas in floods.

If the water is very coloured during these conditions baits such as lobworm, cheese and luncheon meat – all of them having a high degree of smell – can be very good.

Remember that fish do not want to swim around needlessly looking for food. If they can hang around weeds or trees which will provide them with constant food they will do so rather than swimming in open water looking for food. Food will be washed into the slacks during floods, while giving fish a comfortable lie.

Another tell tale sign to look for when rivers are up is an eddy, formed by a slight cut back in the river bank.

CHAPTER SIX

Float fishing

We have already looked briefly at float fishing. Now let's study it more closely.

A float collection any angler would be proud to own but to start with five basic patterns are more than enough.

The floats in your box will be wagglers, antennas, balsas and stick-floats. To start with, a small waggler taking about one swan shot would be ideal for your first trip. Break the shot down as explained earlier, that is, an AA and BB locking the float, two No 4's on the line just over half the depth of the water, and a No 8 a foot from the hook. With only the tip showing this will be heavy enough to cast out and also sensitive enough to show the most delicate bites. Once you can handle your tackle, smaller versions may be used but these won't be so easy to cast or control.

When fishing with a waggler or antenna, which should be attached from the bottom only, always sink your line after casting out. This can bę done by slightly overcasting your mark, placing the rod tip partly under the water and giving a few turns of the reel. The line will sink under the surface and any wind which may be blowing will not affect your tackle.

While fishing with a float of this nature, always keep the rod tip well down while waiting for a bite, to give even greater control over the tackle. If on stillwater your float starts moving along with the wind it means you have not sunk your line properly and the bait is therefore being given an unnatural movement.

All the things I have mentioned so far are the basics. Basic enough for you to catch your first fish but after coming to grips with them, you will need more strings to your bow.

Why fish with a float? It is the most appealing way of catching coarse fish. The visual effect created by a float showing just above the surface of the water gives an exciting air of anticipation. With float gear, baits can be presented much more naturally and on flowing water where your tackle is travelling with the current it allows you to fish otherwise impossible pitches. A float can be trotted (allowed to flow with the current) under overhanging trees – a natural holding spot for fish but sometimes impossible to get to with leger tackle.

The fact that the tackle is constantly on the move also helps search out the fish. You are covering far more ground with your baited hook. Also all depths of the water can be fished. So far I have advocated fishing on or near the bottom but sometimes fish will feed near the surface or midwater.

Start on the bottom and if that doesn't produce results, begin to work your way up in the water, moving the float down the line a few inches at a time.

Which float to use? The smallish waggler I recommend to start with is fine to allow you to get used to fishing with a float but as time goes on you will need to know how to use all the models. Everyone has a favourite float which they use on a certain stretch of water; but just because it works in one swim doesn't mean it will perform the same in another. It is up to you to decide, after finding the depth and the flow, which to employ.

The only hard and fast rules I can give are never use a float, such as a stick or balsa, which has to be attached top and bottom, in still water. Because the float is fixed on the line with two pieces of rubber, one at the top and the other at the bottom of the float the line cannot be sunk.

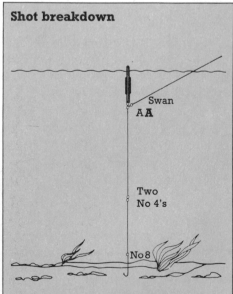

Shot breakdown

Swan
AA

Two
No 4's

No 8

Shot should always be broken down. A 2 swan waggler will work best in deepish water if the shot is split up as shown. This will give better bait presentation and also enable you to cast much further.

So if the slightest ripple ruffles the surface the line and float will automatically move in the same direction giving an unnatural movement to the bait. Small floats – between 2BB and a swan – are perfect for fishing small baits at close range. If, however, you want to fish with bigger baits, such as bread flake or luncheon meat in fastish water, big balsas or sticks are better for the job. Larger wagglers will be needed if you want to cast further. But again remember – put the bulk of the shot around the float.

Try fishing with heavy line and a lightish float and casting will become impossible. Depending on the size of fish you expect, lines should be between 2lb and 4lb, coupled with a finer hook length. The lighter line will cast small and big floats further than the heavy line.

Let's now take a more detailed look at each float mentioned:

With the larger versions you must step up the size of shot slightly but still keep the final shot to a No 8. These floats are most effective for close-in work as the fine stems become difficult to see past 20 yards. A variety from 3BB to 3AA will cope with most conditions.

Slider: There are two versions – the waggler shape and the all balsa type This one is only essential on waters which are very deep – above 12ft. As the name implies, the float is allowed to slide along the line and is only stopped at the correct depth with a sliding knot (see diagram). The knot is tied on to the reel line and can be moved along. If the depth is 18ft then the knot is set at that depth. Unlike all the other shotting patterns mentioned, all the bulk shot – say 3AA – is placed three feet from the hook and in between the bulk and the hook are placed either a BB or No 4, depending on how much shot the float takes.

When you cast out, the slider will be resting above the bulk shot but as the tackle hits the water, the bulk shot will fall to the bottom and cock the float once the knot is trapped in the float's eye. Because the knot used has to be small so as not to restrict casting, the eye on the float has to be smaller still or the knot will go straight through. The waggler type slider has just one eye at the base while the balsa carries two – one at the base and a stand-off one further along the body. The waggler type can be used on both rivers and lakes while the

When fishing in deep water a slider float is a must – but you have to get the stop knot perfect or else the method will present all sorts of problems. The floats work best in depths between 12 ft and 20 ft. The following knot is ideal for sliders:

In cold weather or flood conditions, when fish want a bait anchored on the bottom, laying on is an excellent method. The diagram shows where the shot should be positioned.

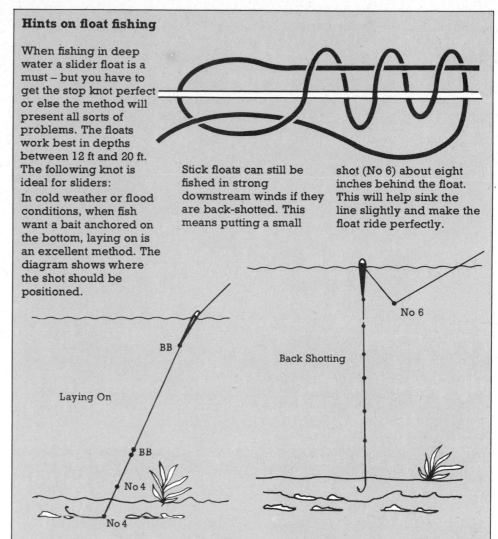

Stick floats can still be fished in strong downstream winds if they are back-shotted. This means putting a small shot (No 6) about eight inches behind the float. This will help sink the line slightly and make the float ride perfectly.

Laying On

BB

BB

No 4

No 4

No 6

Back Shotting

balsa is only suitable for rivers. Always shot the float by using the bulk system as this will cut out tangles and ensure the line is pulled through the float until it reaches the knot.

There are many more floats available than the ones I have mentioned but to go into detail about floats such as zoomers, carrots, avons and duckers will only cause confusion at the outset. All have an important role to play under certain circumstances but once you have mastered the five I have mentioned then handling the others will come naturally.

The shotting patterns I have given are guidelines which will work under most conditions but it is for you to try to find how the fish want the bait presented. It may be that while you are catching fish on the bottom, bites will come quicker on the drop. The theory of float fishing can be picked up from a book but only constant practice will make you a proficient float angler.

Stick float: One of the best floats ever invented for moving waters like the Trent, Thames and Severn. It rides well in the water, having a cane or wire stem and a balsa body. But its uses are also very limited. In a bad wind it becomes difficult to control and maximum range it can be fished, even in perfect conditions, is about four rod lengths out. Designed, therefore, for close-in work, the float is always attached top and bottom with valve rubber. Unlike wagglers, the shot should not be concentrated under the float but spread along the line in "poker" fashion, that is, a 3BB stick should be shotted with a No 1 under the float, a No 4, three No 6's and three No 8's and a micro-dust or another No 8. The largest shot should be under the float and the rest strung out along the line at even intervals.

This gives the bait an even fall. To trot the swim, you need to cast the stick-float rig out, making sure the line is behind the float after it has

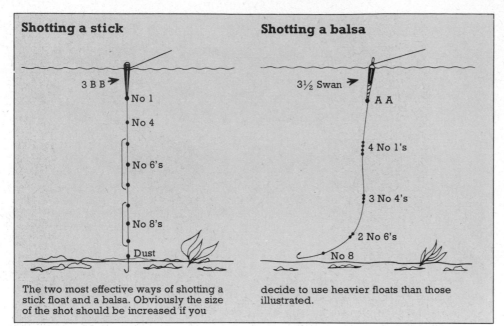

Shotting a stick

3 B B →
No 1
No 4
No 6's
No 8's
Dust

The two most effective ways of shotting a stick float and a balsa. Obviously the size of the shot should be increased if you

Shotting a balsa

3½ Swan →
A A
4 No 1's
3 No 4's
2 No 6's
No 8

decide to use heavier floats than those illustrated.

Waggler on the drop

AA's
No 6
No 8
No 10

A waggler fished on the drop is a method which has really reaped rewards on the River Trent and Thames. Here is a simple shotting pattern for the method.

settled and is starting to flow down with the current. Keep your bail arm open to allow the line to peel off freely. For this method it is obvious that the reel spool should be well backed up so that the line pulls off freely. When you get a bite, put your finger on the spool to trap the line and then strike.

Keep your finger on the spool after the strike and then slowly engage the bail arm, trying not to let any slack line out. It is difficult to avoid a slight decrease in tension when letting your finger off the spool and engaging the bail arm but with a little practice you will soon get the timing correct. While trotting, you can check the line by placing your finger over the reel's open spool. This will stop the float in its tracks and cause the shot and bait to rise in the water, giving it a more appealing motion. If you don't get a bite, once again allow the float

to move freely before checking it further down the swim. Repeating this process along the swim will give a see-saw effect to the bait. Stick-floats are best cast with an underarm motion rather than overhead as this can cause tangles. Anyway you need only flick it out a short distance because you will not be using it for long range work.

Balsa: Another float which is attached top and bottom and for fishing in running water. On a river where the current is very fast and turbulent, a balsa will ride better than a stick. The smaller versions can be shotted in similar fashion to a stick but work better if bunches of two shot are used all the way down the line until the final shot, which should be a single No 8. The heavier ranges are ideal for fishing big baits because of their buoyancy.

On a balsa carrying 3½AA, an AA should be placed under the float, followed by a bunch of four No 1's, a bunch of three No 4's, two No 6's together with a single No 8 – again each bunch should be spaced evenly along the line. This pattern will offset any drag created by the fast water. Again the float is best cast underarm.

Waggler: The most versatile float available which enjoys equal success on rivers and stillwaters (but not stable enough for very fast flowing water). Wagglers are the best float for fishing at long range. The shotting pattern already described for wagglers is a good one to start with but other permutations are available. The shot can be strung on the line the same as for a stick but still with the bulk locking shot around the float. Alternatively baits can be fished "on the drop" (sinking through the water very slowly). This can be achieved by putting all the shot around the float except for a No 6 and two No 8's spaced evenly along the line, with the last shot about 18 inches away from the hook (useful in depth of between four and eight feet). The bait will sink slowly to the bottom and has a good chance of being intercepted on the way by fish feeding in mid-winter.

If you start getting your bait taken without having seen a bite move the last shot nearer the hook or decrease the depth until the bites become clear. Wagglers can be either straight, made from peacock or sarcandas reed, or have a balsa body and the stem from peacock or sarcandas to give them more weight and a greater shot capa-

Angling Times

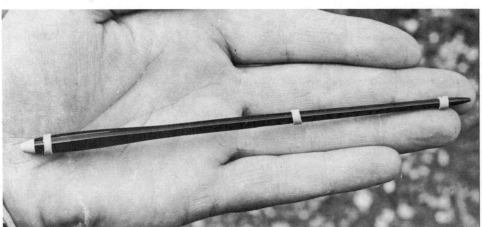

The stick float is the most popular for fishing flowing waters. The one shown takes 3BB and, like all sticks, must be attached top and bottom.

Float fishing helps you present a bait well in the most awkward situations. Here a small roach is swung in between concrete structures.

city. For sensitivity, a small cane insert is often included at the top of the float. Your range should be from 3BB to 5AA.

Holding back

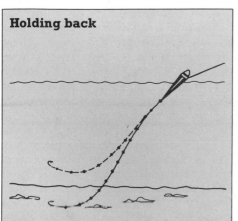

When fishing with a stick float in running water a deadly method can be to hold the tackle back slightly. This will give an appealing lift to the hook bait as it travels down the swim. It will also help catch fish which are feeding just off the bottom.

Antenna: A similar shape to a bodied waggler, but having a thin cane stem. Once the float has been shotted correctly with just a fraction showing, the thin stem will magnify even the most modest bite. Because of their sensitivity, they are ideal floats on canals or stillwater fishing, especially when the fish you are likely to catch are small or shy biting. Some versions have a small brass rod inserted in the bottom making them almost "self-cocking" (standing upright in the water before any shot has been placed on the line). With the built-in weight the minimum of shot is needed on the line. Fished bottom only, these loaded models may need only a No 4 either side to lock them and a few dust shot on the line, a perfect rig for catching rudd and bleak or roach and small bream on the drop. The unloaded versions will take extra locking shot but can still be shotted on the line in the same way.

Loaded antenna

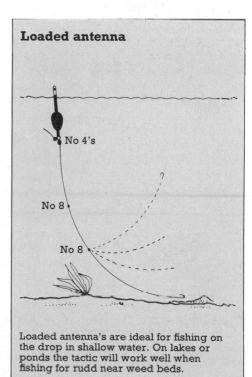

No 4's

No 8

No 8

Loaded antenna's are ideal for fishing on the drop in shallow water. On lakes or ponds the tactic will work well when fishing for rudd near weed beds.

CHAPTER SEVEN

Leger fishing

Legering is a method of catching coarse fish without the use of a float to help you register the bite.

Instead of putting shot on the line a leger weight is tied to the bottom of the reel line and then the hook length added. Because the leger will sink your bait is always fished on the bottom when using this tactic.

In the past, legering was always considered a chuck it and chance it method, requiring less dexterity than float fishing, but in the past ten years it has really come into its own, producing some spectactular results which would never have been possible on float rigs.

And the reason legering has now become an accepted form of fishing is because of the invention of various bite indicators. The two most popular indicators are swingtips and quivertips, which will signal bites from a fish when legering. These will screw into the end eye of the rod, the line will be threaded through the rod and also through the eyes on the indicators – making the indicator a sensitive extension of the rod.

If the float rod you bought has an end eye with a screw-in fitting it can be used for legering (or you can ask your tackle dealer to fit one for you) but ideally you now need to buy another rod – one designed specifically for bottom fishing.

These are normally between nine and ten feet long having a through action rather than a tip action favoured on the float rods. The through action gives you greater striking and casting power.

Before explaining all the intricate details of legering, let's have a look at the advantages of fishing a bait on the bottom without the use of a float:

1. Leger weights are much heavier than the amount of shot you would

When a bream shoal really starts to feed it can mean all systems go. Here two anglers play bream at the same time.

place on a normal sized float. Therefore greater distances can be cast. This is an advantage when you know that the spot where the fish are feeding is further out than can be comfortably reached with float gear.

On lakes it may be that there is a deep gully 30 yards out where the fish prefer to lie. On rivers the far banks may be the place where natural holding spots, such as overhanging trees and bushes, are to be found.

2. Many fish, especially bream, prefer to feed on the bottom. Legering will get the bait down to the fish much more quickly and present it in a way which is more appealing to them.

3. In very windy conditions it can be almost impossible for a beginner to fish comfortably with float tackle. Strong gusts can play havoc with float control so to fish the bait as natural as possible legering is often the answer.

4. In very deep water legering is easier than fishing with a sliding float. It will ensure your bait reaches the

bottom every time.

5. Very fast water can present problems to newcomers when float fishing. The float is being carried down the river so quickly that the tackle becomes difficult to control. In cases such as this legering will overcome the problem.

6. Rivers are likely to flood in winter. The water will be coloured and running at a faster pace than normal. Allowing your bait to trot along with the current in the coloured water will make it difficult for the fish to see the bait. A bait fished on the bottom is more likely to pick up fish.

7. During very cold spells fish prefer to lie dormant on the bottom. If your bait is cast near them and kept on the bottom they are much more inclined to pick the bait up than if it is trotted past them.

8. It is much easier to fish bigger baits, such as bread, luncheon meat paste or cheese with leger tackle than it is with float gear.

The above points are the main

Setting up leger rigs

The following three methods can be used to fix leger weights on the line. The running leger tends to be less sensitive. The running paternoster is not advisable in weedy areas as the stop shot and swivel pick up debris. The favorite and most effective is the straight paternoster.

Straight Leger → To Reel
Stop Shot
Arlesey Bomb

Stop Shot → To Reel
Two-eyed Swivel
Running Paternoster
Arlesey Bomb

Hook-link tied to loop in reel line by a half blood-knot → To Reel
Straight Paternoster
Arlesey Bomb

reasons you would fish with leger tackle. Legering presents another dimension to your angling skills and can mean the difference between nothing or having a bonanza.

Having bought a leger rod or adapted your float rod, which indicator should you buy?

Before bite indicators were invented, the three main ways of detecting that a fish had taken the bait while legering were – watching the rod tip, holding the line and feeling for bites or placing something like a dough bobbin on the line. All these were less effective than today's modern gadgets.

I well remember legering for carp on my local canal as a ten-year-old. There, on the concrete banks, I would set up an "alarm" system while legering with cheese. The rod would lie along the bank on two wooden rests and, once the line had been tightened up to the leger, following the cast, I would balance a halfpenny on the end of the rod top. Underneath was placed a metal lid so on any sudden tap the coin would clatter on to the lid – registering the bite.

This crude rig worked but I often think how much better my results would have been had today's legering

aids been thought of. Besides, with really hard bites the coin would often spin into the canal, making it a bit hard on the pocket money.

We have come a long way since then. The swing-tips and quiver-tips now available will pick up the slightest tremble. Your aim when legering should be to make sure that when a fish picks up your bait it cannot feel any resistance on the line. At the same time you want to be able to spot the bite.

Compare it to float fishing. There you have the float shotted down very finely so that the fish cannot feel anything when it takes the float under. You see the bite and strike. Your legering tactics should be on the same lines.

Swing-tip: This is normally a piece of light cane with two small eyes – one at the end and one near the top. At the top there should be a small length of rubber attached to the cane. And at the other end of the rubber a screw-in adaptor which will fit into the end eye of your rod. When attached, the swing-tip will hang down from the rod and the rubber fitting will allow it to move about freely. After screwing the tip into the rod and threading the line through it, the cast should be a smooth, steady one so as not to jerk the rod and cause the swing-tip to bounce about too much. If it does bounce, the line can become tangled and impair the cast. Worse still the sudden resistance can cause the line to snap.

After casting out, you must sink the line from your leger to the end of the swing-tip (the same as when float fishing). This is done by reeling in the slack line until it is tight to the leger weight. Put the rod in the rest – which should be placed so that when the swing-tip is allowed to hang down it just touches the surface of the water. If, after putting the rod in the rest, there is still slack line, wind in the extra line which will cause the tip to move upwards until it is tight. Release a fraction of line from the reel so the tip just hangs on the surface. A bite will be registered by the tip either moving upwards or dropping back (always set the tip at a slight angle so that if the line to the leger goes slack it will drop back a fraction). The drop back bite is caused when the fish has picked up the bait and starts to swim towards you making the leger move off the bottom.

Always buy swing-tips which are between eight and 12 inches long. These will allow a fish to swim further

Swinging the lead

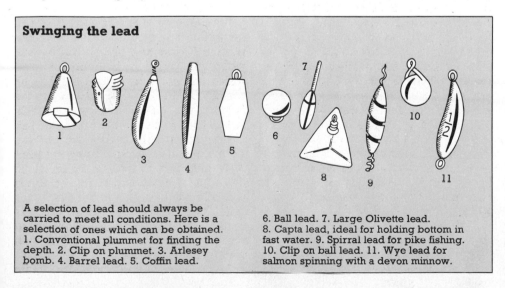

A selection of lead should always be carried to meet all conditions. Here is a selection of ones which can be obtained. 1. Conventional plummet for finding the depth. 2. Clip on plummet. 3. Arlesey bomb. 4. Barrel lead. 5. Coffin lead. 6. Ball lead. 7. Large Olivette lead. 8. Capta lead, ideal for holding bottom in fast water. 9. Spiral lead for pike fishing. 10. Clip on ball lead. 11. Wye lead for salmon spinning with a devon minnow.

with the bait before any resistance is felt. Resistance will be felt only once the tip has risen up to its limit so it is advisable to strike while it is on its way up. For still waters buy light tips but if you are fishing a river which has a slight movement the drag from the current will mean that a heavier tip is needed to ensure it hangs in the correct position. Small pieces of lead wire can be wound round the end of the tip to counteract any flow. For fast running water a quiver-tip must be used.

Quiver-tips: These are usually around eight inches long with a screw-in adaptor in one end and an eye at the other. They are usually tapered for greater sensitivity. The basics of tightening the line up after a cast are the same as when using a swing-tip. Settle the tip until there is a very slight bend in it. Bites will again either pull the tip round or make it drop back. Quiver-tips will take the strain of the current yet still let you see the bites. For very fast water you want a stiffish quiver and for waters such as the Trent, one which is moderately stiff. They have several advantages over the swing-tip in that they are not affected by the wind, are easier to cast with and can be fished under any conditions.

While swing-tips and quiver-tips have made tremendous improvements to legering there are two MUSTS which have to be mastered – ground-baiting and casting. The two go hand in hand.

If your intention is to fish 30 yards out, that is where you will place your groundbait. At the same time it is common sense that this is where you will be casting your leger, complete with baited hook. The groundbait is put there to attract fish and to make them feed, so you want the "business end" of the tackle to be there as well. Looked at in human terms, if you have a group of people eating in the dining room and you want to catch one it is pointless casting into the lounge. The only ones which will come across your bait are those that are leaving the dining room – already full up. The same goes for fish.

Groundbaiting on big open waters can be confusing. It's easy to forget exactly where you placed it, therefore the secret is to find a marker on the opposite bank, say a tree. Line up the range you are fishing at with the marker and stick to that area. Cast into the same area and you can fish confidently, knowing your bait is in the right place.

When legering for the first time pick a distance where you can throw your groundbait and cast without too much effort. Remember that by making things easy for yourself you will always have a much more enjoyable day. Try going too far before you have really mastered the method and you could be in for a very frustrating day.

Striking: When legering, the strike should be made once the indicator you are using has made a positive move. The best bites are obviously those which just sail upwards or pull the tip round. Sometimes, however, especially with bream, the indicator will move only a fraction but hold there. Those sort of bites should always be struck. I recommend leaving any small knocks or taps. But be on the look-out for any drop-back bites; they should always be struck firmly. The strike should be a quick steady motion, following the rod round until you can feel the fish. When fishing a long way out it may be necessary to strike a little harder to make sure you pick up all the line.

Line bites: If you have cast a long way out – say 30 yards – you will have that amount of line underneath the water between your leger and the end or your indicator. So it stands to reason that if a fish swims along the path of your line and touches it, the movement will be registered on the indicator. This is known as a false bite or line bite.

When a big bream shoal is in your swim, the indicator can sometimes be constantly moving as the fish swim around the bottom. For beginners it is difficult to appreciate what is happening. The natural reaction is to keep on striking but this will only unsettle the shoal – they will become scared as the leger weight is pulled past or into them time after time. Line bites are easier to pick out with a swing-tip. If you have already stuck at a couple of "bites" which haven't marked your bait leave the next one until the tip goes right up. If the tip goes halfway up and then drops back into its normal position, it is odds-on that it is a line bite. If the tip goes up and keeps going

Hints on legering for carp

All night carp and tench sessions can be cold even on a summer's evening. Anglers must keep warm or else their concentration will start to wander. Camp beds with plenty of blankets or a sleeping bag is a better idea than sitting on a basket all night. Umbrellas with windbreaks round them make ideal make shift bankside "homes".

Floating crust is difficult to cast. If you fish a shallow swim a leger can be used to aid the cast. Say the swim is four feet deep you need to have a trace of more than four feet. After the cast has been made the bomb will lay on the bottom while the crust will float on the surface.

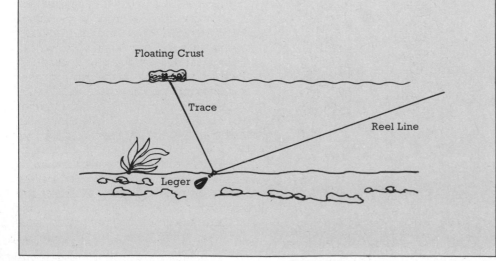

or holds there, strike – for that will be a positive bite. Coping effectively with this type of situation can only be done with experience, but it does pay to cast short when line bites keep persisting.

Which leger to use: The arlesey bomb is by far the best. The size of the leger you tie on will depend very much on the distance out you want to fish and the strength of the current. For short casts in still water a "bomb" of ¼oz will be sufficient but for casts of 30 yards one of ½oz or ¾oz will be needed. Again in fast water the size will have to be stepped up so that the leger remains firmly anchored to the bottom. In very fast water coffin leads or capta leads will hold better than arlesey bombs because of their shape. *(See diagram on the three best ways of attaching legers to your line and tying on the hook length.)*

Hook lengths: In still water the hook length should be around four feet. This will give a fish time to pick up your bait and take it before feeling any resistance from the "bomb". Long hook lengths also allow the bait to fall slowly through the last few feet of the swim, giving you a chance of catching on the drop. In faster water you need a smaller hook length to ensure the bait is not fluttering around way off the bottom. But do not take these as rigid rules. If you find you have had a bite with a long hook length

and not seen it then it may be that the length needs to be shortened so the bite can be registered more quickly. Very quick bites can often be turned into strikable bites by increasing the hook length.

Hook sizes: The guide lines I gave earlier in the book also apply to legering. Hook sizes should always be linked with the strength of line you are using and the bait you use.

Target Boards: These are used to help pick out timid bites usually in windy conditions. The two illustrated are the most common for swing-tipping and quiver-tipping. Some tackle shops sell them but they can be easily made out of a piece of perspex, and painted with mat black paint.

Swimfeeders: These have added a completely new dimension to legering. Swimfeeders come in two patterns – open ended and block end. They are tied on the line in place of a leger and filled with either groundbait or maggots, ensuring that your baited hook is always near your feed. The open-ended version is for groundbait. Pack the groundbait and some hook bait into the feeder and cast out. It is most effective in still or slow moving water since the groundbait will stay in the area you have cast and not be carried along the bottom.

The block end type has a series of holes drilled in the plastic casing

When using a swing tip or a quiver always use a steady, sweeping sideways strike.

(both models are usually made of thin plastic) and a plastic cap at each end. At the end which is tied to the reel line the cap is detachable so that it can be lifted off and filled with maggots and then replaced. After the maggot-filled feeder has been cast out, the maggots will escape through the holes and cause a steady trickle of bait along the swim. Fish will start feeding on the free offerings and move towards where they are coming from – and hopefully pick up your baited hook on their way. Blockends are best on flowing water.

The swimfeeder has enabled novices to boost their catches because it eliminates the skills of groundbaiting accurately. Wherever you cast your hookbait will always be near your feed but a must when "feedering" is to cast into the same spot each time to concentrate the feed in a small area – and at the same time to get the fish into that confined area. Cast all over the place and the fish will spread themselves out looking for the bait.

For feeder fishing you will need to fish with around 4lb reel line to allow you to cast out without snapping your line. The feeders when full can weigh several ounces but once they have emptied there isn't too much resistance.

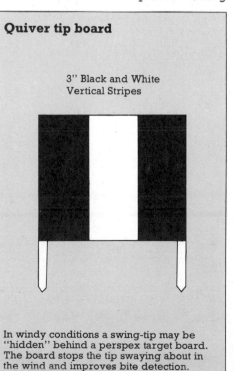

Swingtip target board

Rod Tip Rests here with
Swintip Hanging Behind Shield

Clear Perspex
"Dial"

When fish are very shy biting a target board as shown becomes very useful while quiver tipping. The end of the tip can be matched up with one of the lines showing the slightest movement of the tip.

Quiver tip board

3" Black and White
Vertical Stripes

In windy conditions a swing-tip may be "hidden" behind a perspex target board. The board stops the tip swaying about in the wind and improves bite detection.

CHAPTER EIGHT

Pike fishing

Pike are predators feeding on small fish such as roach, rudd, dace, bleak, gudgeon and skimmer bream.

Therefore if you are going to set out with pike in mind your aim should be to use either live or dead fish as bait or simulate a small fish by using a spinner or plug. Pike, contrary to the opinion of many anglers, are not difficult to catch but, as in all forms of fishing, the approach must be correct.

Most waters contain pike but the size of the fish will vary according to the environment in which they live. A large lake with plenty of "small fry" for pike to feed on will produce big fish. This is why the big landlocked Irish and Scottish waters come up with huge pike each year. A small pond or canal, however, is unlikely to hold a large head of 20lb plus pike. Fish of 15lb can be regarded as an excellent catch.

Many anglers devote all their time to pike fishing. They are specialists and, having studied this form of fishing in greater detail than most anglers, have developed their own methods to catch a larger share of the specimen fish. My aim in this chapter is to try to make you familiar with the basics of pike fishing – giving you a foundation of knowledge on which to build. For excitement you don't have to land a huge pike first time out. A fish of 4lb will put up enough struggle to make you want to try again.

Tackle: The float rod you have is no good for pike fishing. It is just not strong enough to cast out live or dead baits and not powerful enough to land a biggish pike. Ideally you need another rod, something like a fast taper 10ft or 11ft pike rod, which will cope with most situations. But as most youngsters have limits on what they can spend on tackle I would suggest

A 6lb pike safely in the net. Live or dead baiting is by far the most successful methods for pike.

that the 10ft leger rod you should have obtained by now will cope for starters. Use the same open-faced reel you would use for float or leger fishing but load the spool – or buy an extra spool – with 8lb line. Other items of tackle are wire traces, barbless treble hooks from size 12's to 6's, a pike float, some barrel, spiral or wye leads, and an assortment of spinners and plugs. A pair of forceps and a pike gag will be needed to remove the hook from the fish you catch.

Before I explain the three most common methods for pike fishing let me emphasise one point – make sure the water you visit contains a good head of pike. This can be done by either reading the angling press for reports of big pike catches or asking your local tackle dealer or angling club secretary.

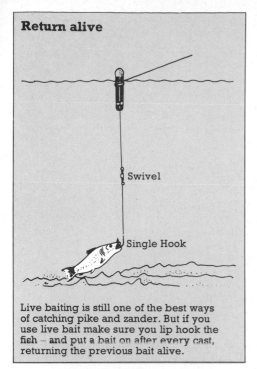

Return alive

Swivel

Single Hook

Live baiting is still one of the best ways of catching pike and zander. But if you use live bait make sure you lip hook the fish – and put a bait on after every cast, returning the previous bait alive.

Live-baiting: This, in my opinion, is the easiest and best method for you to catch your first pike. The bait is a completely natural one and therefore more tempting to a hungry pike. You will need the pike float – which should vary in size according to how big a live-bait you will be using – the lead weight and the wire trace and treble hook. The wire trace should have a swivel on it to stop the line from kinking and should be about three foot long. Remember pike have rows of needle sharp teeth which can cut through the thickest nylon line. The trace breaking strain needs to be around 8–10lb.

In the winter it is advisable to take your live-baits (say small gudgeon and roach) with you when lake fishing. You can often catch live-baits from a river in winter when it is impossible to catch them from stillwaters.

The baits should be kept in a large bucket or plastic container, preferably with a lid with air holes punched in it. Once you are at the water's edge put the fish into a keep net. In the summer live-baits can often be caught easily enough if it is a well stocked lake.

As mentioned earlier, the float needs to be fairly big to carry the live-bait and the lead weight without going under. The lead weight is to help you keep the live-bait down in the water – without it the fish tend to swim towards the surface. Set the tackle a few feet off the bottom, take out a live-bait and either lip-hook it with the treble or place the treble in its back. I prefer to lip-hook the baits because

it causes them less harm. Two trebles can be used – one set in the lip and the other just in front of the dorsal fin. With this method you are less likely to throw off your bait on the cast.

Look for any natural holding areas before making your first cast. Pike like to lie near weeds or in the deeper gullies of gravel pits and lakes. Don't try to cast too far, just make a nice steady forward cast without jerking the tackle. A cast of 20 yards should be ample to get you near some sort of natural holding area.

The bite: When pike fishing the bite is called "a run", the time when the pike has made off with your bait. Unlike coarse fishing for roach, bream and so on, pike should not be struck immediately. They need time to take hold of the bait, and swim along to turn it. You will have the excitement of seeing the pike float suddenly being pulled under – the pike has taken the bait. Leave your bail arm open to allow the line to run off freely. The line will start to peel off as the fish swims away with the bait. Leave it until the fish has stopped and then starts to run again.

This is the time to strike. The pike has turned the bait. With small baits such as gudgeon or bleak, pike can be struck earlier but it is a question of practice. The strike should be made only after you have reeled in any slack line you may have between your rod and the fish. Once the line tightens, lean your rod back into the fish with a good, firm follow-through strike. Another strike can be made to make

doubly sure the hooks are well set.

Play the fish carefully to the net. If you have struck too soon the pike will let go of the bait without being hooked. If the bait is still on, cast out immediately for pike will often have another go at the bait that has been snatched away from them.

Unhooking: The gag, a metal device, is used to force the pike's jaws open so the hooks can be removed safely with the aid of forceps. The two ends of the gag which go into the pike's mouth should be bound with rag or tape so as not to damage the fish's mouth. Keep the fish still and remove the hooks carefully. If the hooks have been completely swallowed cut the trace as near to the hooks as possible and return the fish. All pike should be returned unless you intend to eat your catch.

Deadbaiting: Again this method entails the use of small fish but this time they are dead. While roach and so on can be used, most anglers prefer to fish with sprats, herrings or mackerel bought from a fishmonger. I would recommend sprats to start with as the other two fish are heavier and therefore more difficult to cast out. Herrings and mackerel are usually used when big fish are sought.

Dead-baits are best fished on the bottom with legering tactics. The line and tackle is almost identical minus the float. Use an arlesey bomb of around ¾oz. Put this on your main line and then tie on the trace – this time two hooks are best (shop bought snap-

Big wide open waters such as Scottish and Irish lakes are more likely to produce specimen pike than small ponds or rivers.

Fillets

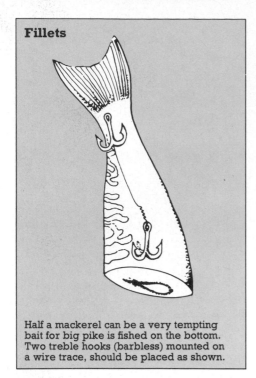

Half a mackerel can be a very tempting bait for big pike is fished on the bottom. Two treble hooks (barbless) mounted on a wire trace, should be placed as shown.

tackle can be employed). The bottom hook should be placed in the dead fish's side about half-way along and the top hook just along from its tail. The fish should now be hanging upside down when you make the cast. Fish the same areas you would with live-bait.

When the cast has been made, place your rod in a rest and leave the bail arm open. If there is no flow on the water, place a small piece of silver paper over the line between the reel and the butt ring. If the water is pulling use a heavier form of indicator, such as a dough bobbin. The run will be spotted by the indicator moving up-wards and the line peeling off. Follow the same procedure with the strike as you would with live-baiting.

Spinning: Plugs and spinners are known as lures. Spinners are made out of metal while plugs are either wooden or plastic. When cast out both will simulate fish swimming through the water when they are reeled in. The plugs you should have are those which float and dive. There are hundreds of patterns of spinners but proven ones include Mepps, Vibro, Droppen or Toby.

When spinning an anti-kink vane should be fitted on to the reel line – which can be dropped down to 6lb – before tying on the trace and spinner. The trace should have a quick release clip on the end so lures can be changed if need be. The lures should be fished nearer the surface in summer and

deeper during the colder months.

The retrieve of the spinner is all important. Wind it back too slowly and you may be catching the bottom all the while – too fast and a pike may not have time to grab it. The retrieve should be a nice steady one. With lure fishing you can "work-out" a stretch of river or lake. Cast, say to your left and reel in; now cast slightly to the right of your first spot and so on. In this way an arc can be covered. Once you come to the end of the arc to your right, either repeat the process or move to another area until you get a take.

The take will usually just stop your retrieve, keep the line tight and just lift the rod into the fish. Don't strike viciously for you may snatch the lure out of the pike's mouth. With lure fishing pike are usually hooked in the side of the jaws.

At the end of each retrieve lift the spinner or plug from the water gently for often a pike will follow the lure all the way into the bank and take it just as you are lifting out.

Trace the line

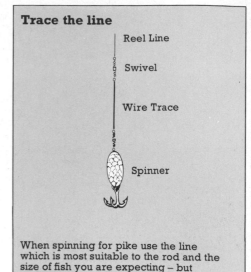

Reel Line

Swivel

Wire Trace

Spinner

When spinning for pike use the line which is most suitable to the rod and the size of fish you are expecting – but always have a short wire trace. Pike have a mouth full of sharp teeth which can easily bite through nylon.

The exciting thing about spinning for pike is that you never know how big the fish will be that grabs your lure. It could be a tiny jack pike or a double figure fish like this beauty.

When pike fishing you should always be looking to cast your spinner or livebait into the natural habitat of pike. Water lilies like these or weed beds make ideal cover for a hungry pike.

CHAPTER NINE

Trout fishing

Trout fishing used to be regarded as a sport for the rich. But now, since hundreds of reservoirs and lakes have been artificially stocked with trout, a whole new and exciting world has become available – stillwater trout fishing.

A wide selection of artificial flies are handy to have but lures such as sweeney todds are always good at the start of the season.

This branch of the sport is still booming. Each year new waters are added to the list of "put and take" fisheries (waters where the owners put back as many trout as have been taken).

And the beauty with stillwater trout fishing is that unlike most river fishing for trout, where a fish of 1lb is considered a good fish, these waters are stocked with quality rainbow and brown trout.

The big waters, such as Rutland, Draycott, Grafham and Pitsford, normally receive stocking of trout of at least 1lb and many smaller waters such as Avington and Church Hill Farm regularly place them in as big as 10lb.

Most of Britain's stillwater trout fisheries are day ticket ones – usually giving concessionary permits to juniors – most offering excellent value for money.

Fly fishing, however, is completely different from either coarse or sea fishing and therefore a complete new set of specialised tackle is required. Like the other forms of fishing it pays in the long term to buy the best kit you can possibly afford. Here is a list of the tackle you need to cope with any reservoir or lake in the country.

Rod: A good glass fibre rod with plenty of action – but not too sloppy – is what you are looking for. It should take a number eight fly line to give you the maximum casting distance.

Line: Fly lines are not like any other lines used for coarse or sea fishing. Fly lines are thick, either having a forward taper or double taper in them. The reason for their thickness is that with fly fishing you do not have a weight on to help you cast – the only aid to casting is the weight of the line.

It is most important that the line should balance your rod so if you get a rod taking a number eight line that is the size of line you MUST have.

There are three different types of full line – sinking, floating and sink-tip. They do exactly what their names suggest, with the sink-tip being made of a floating line with the last ten feet of the line sinking.

At the end of your fly line should be attached a leader of 14lb–20lb nylon line and on to this is tied your trace, on to which you put the fly.

Reel: The least important item. Unlike coarse and sea fishing the reel does not help you cast – it is merely there to hold your line on when not in use.

Other essentials are a selection of wet flies (ones which sink), a landing net, waders, shoulder-bag to carry your tackle in and a Priest – a small truncheon like aid to kill your catch.

So how do you catch a trout? The object is simple – you cast your artificial fly out into the lake or reservoir, let it sink slightly and then start to retrieve. When you come almost to the end of the fly line, lift it gently off the surface and repeat the process.

In reality it is much harder to catch your first trout. The thing which is probably the hardest to come to terms with at the outset is casting. Learning to cast can be done on the bankside but I would recommend a few practice sessions (without a fly on) in your local park. You will learn even more quickly if an experienced caster can show you the rudiments. It will seem difficult at first but it is only a matter of timing.

When you are a beginner, watch the line both on the back cast and the forward cast. Your aim will be to get the line going backwards and forwards through the air – letting a bit more out on each forward cast.

Once the line has straightened out at the back, then start the forward cast. The rod should always be going between ten and two on a clock face. Drop the rod too far back and you will catch the bank behind you. It is much easier to describe the cast with a sequence of drawings, so look at these step-by-step shots and try to imitate them. One secret when learning to cast is to use your full arm not just your wrist.

When buying your tackle ask the dealer to wind the fly line on to your reel and also to tie on the leader. To start with a sinking line or sink-tip will cope with most circumstances although in the summer when fish start to rise freely on the surface you would be advised to invest in a floating line. Buying all three is expensive but they are needed.

A small selection of wet flies – Peter Ross, Black Lure, Mallard and Claret, Sweeney Todd, Butcher, and Invicta are some of the common patterns – will obviously be needed.

The ones I have mentioned are fine to start with but as you visit a water more freely local anglers will put you in the picture as to which patterns prove most effective during certain months.

At the water: Set your tackle up and tie on to the end of the leader a length of 6lb nylon – about ten feet at first. On to this tie your fly (at the beginning of the season something like a Sweeney Todd or Black Lure will be ideal). Flick about ten feet of fly line on to the water and start your cast.

Don't be too ambitious at first. A cast of 15 yards will be fine. Remember if you are right-handed choose a spot where the wind is blowing from left to right so your line is blown away from your body. This will cut down the risk of you hooking yourself. If you are left-handed you will need to find a place with the opposite conditions.

Rivers and small streams often hold "wild" brown trout but they tend to be a much smaller stamp than those found in reservoirs.

Having cast, you then need to retrieve the fly. This is done by pulling the line in by hand. Trap the line between your forefinger and thumb of the hand holding your rod, and then pull line in with the other hand. Pull the line a full arm's length at a time – using a nice, gentle pace. If this speed of retrieve does not produce a fish after about 20 casts try speeding up the retrieve or slowing it down. Often it is a case of trial and error in finding out how a trout wants the fly presented.

Never snatch the fly off the water when you go to recast. Often a fish will follow your fly right in and take

The correct way to hold the rod and line when starting the retrieve.

it just as you are about to lift off. It is really exciting when you see the fish take the fly.

If a trout takes your fly while it is well out from the bank do not strike. As you feel the heart-stopping pull of the fish when it seizes your fly just lift the rod into it and keep the pressure on.

Don't try and bully the fish to the bank. If it wants to run, let it, but keep a slight arc in your rod at all times. The slack line is best retrieved by hand – just the same as you do when retrieving the line after a cast.

Trout, especially rainbows, will sometimes make spectacular leaps out of the water, in a bid to shake out the hook, so it is important to keep in contact with the fish throughout the fight.

Once safely in the net, take it up the bank and using your Priest give it a good, sharp bang on the head. Few waters stock with undersized fish so the ones you catch can safely be taken home. The minimum size is usually around 12 inches. Waters do have a limit on the amount you can take with you – this varies from four to eight though a few waters, such as Packington and Eyebrook, have no limits.

As you become more experienced your casting will improve; you will start learning which flies to use by talking to local anglers, and you will quickly find the hot spots.

What to look for: Unlike coarse fishing groundbaiting is not allowed when fly fishing so there is no way of making the fish feed or attracting them into your pitch. You have to find the fish.

If the fish are feeding on the surface and therefore rising they are easy to spot but in colder weather trout tend to feed well down. First try your sinking line along the bottom by allowing plenty of time for the line to sink through the water. If this doesn't work, start the retrieve a little sooner and so on. By varying the amount of time you give the line to sink you can explore all the depths of the water and with luck, find at which level the fish are feeding.

In windy conditions you can spot trout feeding below the waves by studying the water carefully. You may only see a slight swirl or change in a wave but it will signal a fish. Cast your fly to where you saw the fish and then start the retrieve immediately. Fish will congregate along areas

Nymph fishing and casting

Nymphs need to be pulled back slowly. The ideal retrieve is the figure of eight where the line is collected in your left hand (if you are right handed). By keeping up a steady retrieve the nymphs can be pulled back naturally.

Roll cast. Feed out about 15 ft of line with the rod tip at eye level. Raise rod to one o'clock position, cast forwards strongly – the belly of line should be slightly behind right elbow – to pull rest of

extended line from water. Rod moves right through past 9 o'clock position. Fly will roll up and over. When the line is straight out the fly will touch the water first.

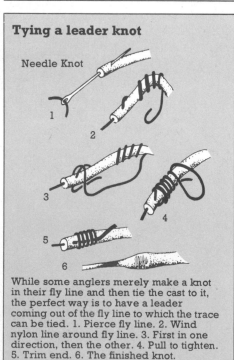

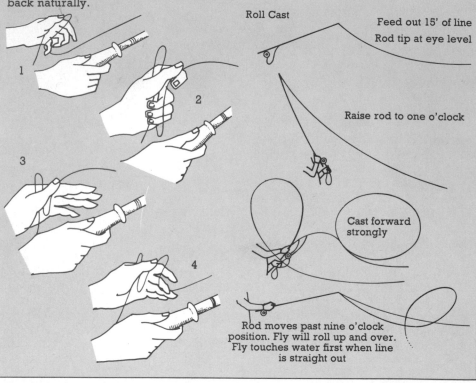

Roll Cast

Feed out 15' of line
Rod tip at eye level

Raise rod to one o'clock

Cast forward strongly

Rod moves past nine o'clock position. Fly will roll up and over. Fly touches water first when line is straight out

Tying a leader knot

Needle Knot

1
2
3
4
5
6

While some anglers merely make a knot in their fly line and then tie the cast to it, the perfect way is to have a leader coming out of the fly line to which the trace can be tied. 1. Pierce fly line. 2. Wind nylon line around fly line. 3. First in one direction, then the other. 4. Pull to tighten. 5. Trim end. 6. The finished knot.

Parts of a nymph

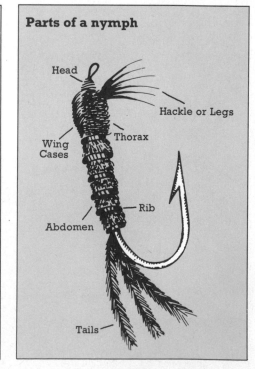

Head

Hackle or Legs

Wing Cases

Thorax

Rib

Abdomen

Tails

where the wind is blowing into the bank. It is difficult to cast into the wind, especially if it is a strong one, but this sort of perseverance will usually pay off handsomely.

As you become more experienced, an enjoyable spin-off from fly fishing is tying your own flies. Once you have bought the materials needed flies can be tied for just a few pence.

Once casting has been mastered and you become familiar with the different patterns of flies and which lines to use in certain conditions, fly fishing becomes very much a personal thing. You will develop your own favourite flies – ones you always seem to have success with. On any day of the season at any popular water, if you asked ten successful anglers which flies they had used I can guarantee most of them have used different patterns. So pick the ones you have the greatest confidence in.

Probably the best tip I ever received on fly fishing was: "Keep your flies in the water". It is difficult to keep going through the motions, especially when you haven't had a single take or no fish are rising. But if you are resting on the bank you have no chance of catching.

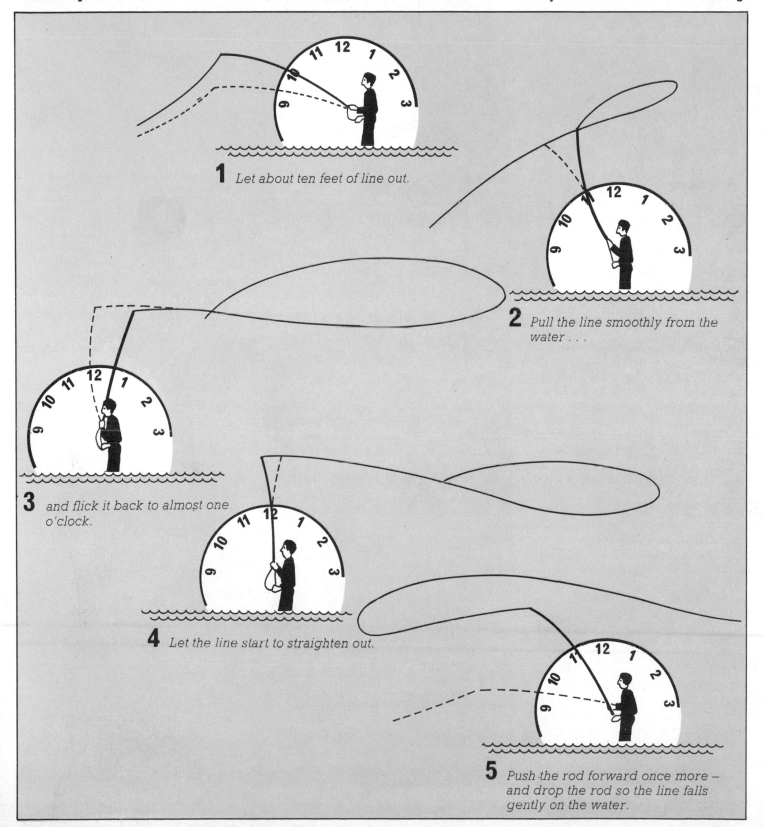

1 *Let about ten feet of line out.*

2 *Pull the line smoothly from the water . . .*

3 *and flick it back to almost one o'clock.*

4 *Let the line start to straighten out.*

5 *Push the rod forward once more – and drop the rod so the line falls gently on the water.*

CHAPTER TEN

Canals and small stream fishing

Canals and small streams are two waterways which are often neglected by the more serious angler but which can be great fun for beginners.

Canals can be very rewarding but the fish, generally roach, perch, bream and gudgeon tend to be small.

Canals: These are man-made waterways and are normally shallow (around four feet) and clear, depending on how much boat traffic uses them. They can be tremendous training grounds. Once you can regularly catch fish from canals you will be able to cope with the shyest of fish.

Because canals are shallow, and not very wide the fish are easily scared so the approach needs to be a delicate one. Small hooks (size 20 or 22) little baits such as pinkies or punched bread and small antenna floats. The antenna should take around 2BB and only a dust shot on the line. This should be placed around half-way between the float and hook to allow the bait to fall naturally through the water. On canals most fish will take the bait on the drop.

Canals usually have two "shelves". One on the far bank and one under the rod end with the deeper boat channel running down the middle. The far shelf is a good bet for roach while the deeper channel will hold roach, gudgeon and bream. The near shelf, especially if fringed with weed, will produce roach, perch, gudgeon and tench. As with the tackle the feeding pattern should also be delicate – just a few loose fed pinkies and a grape-sized spot of very soft groundbait in the area you are fishing every now and again.

Tackle up well away from the bank and try to choose a swim which has high reeds on your bank so you can hide yourself behind them. Remember the fish can easily be spooked if there is too much commotion on the bank.

Streams: When I was a youngster I spent many worthwhile hours fishing tiny streams – waters you wouldn't have believed could hold fish. Yet swims of only a foot deep produced dace and roach. As in canal fishing, you need to be delicate and well-hidden. With streams you can often see the fish swimming around if you

Canal composition

Match fishing canal can be rewarding providing you know the contours of the "cut". Canal weights are usually low so you need to pick up as many fish as possible. The first ledge – apparent in most canals – will hold shoals of gudgeon or small roach while the second and far ledge is more suitable for roach and bream. Concentrate on these ledges before going into the middle.

In fast water shop bought swim feeders are not always heavy enough to hold bottom. Extra strips of lead can be added but a simple way to increase the 'feeders weight is to fix a nut and bolt through the bottom. Small, circular lead discs can also be added to the bolt, if the current increases still further.

First Ledge

Second Ledge

are quiet enough and can therefore "stalk" them – see the fish and cast the bait to them.

Use a small balsa float (2BB) but fish it only from the bottom if the water is very shallow. Place 1BB and a No 4 under the float and a No 4 halfway between hook and float. Use 18 or 16 hooks for chub. Quality roach are always on the cards with this style of fishing. Double maggot or caster or a small worm are excellent baits. If you see a shoal of fish, creep a few yards upstream and start loose feeding with casters or maggots, just a dozen at a time until you see the fish become interested. Cast your float above the fish and let it trot down. Bites in fast shallow water will pull the float right under or take it across the current. The strike should be sideways in shallow swims because it will cause less disturbance and if you do miss the bite the chances of the tackle tangling are reduced.

Deeper holes are often found in streams and these can be fished with the "top and bottom" style mentioned earlier. These holes are a good bet for perch, chub, roach and even the occasional bream.

When fishing streams always stick to loose feeding rather than throwing in groundbait. This will only scare the fish.

A typical canal fish – a tiny roach. Fish of this size are very common on Britain's chain of canals. While no records are likely to be broken fished for with delicate tackle they can provide hours of fun.

Canals provide very fair venues for match fishing. Here an angler fishing a juvenile contest puts float tactics to good use finishing with a net of small bream and roach. His 4lb catch is a good weight for a canal.

Sea fishing, our next chapter, is always exciting because of the variety of fish you can expect. Our pictures show a group of youngsters displaying their catch of small wrasse, pollack and rockling, (top) the size of fish you can expect (bottom left) and a junior angler trying his luck from the shore (bottom right).

CHAPTER ELEVEN

Sea fishing - shore and boat

Sea fishing, whether from a beach, off rocks or piers or from a boat, can be one of the most exciting forms of angling. Fishing with even the crudest tackle, you always have a chance of catching something – and the wait for a bite is made even more interesting because you never know exactly what type of fish could pick up your baited hook.

You may set out just to try for a few flat-fish when a hard-fighting bass comes along and takes your bait. Boat fishing over war-time wrecks can give all kinds of unexpected excitement if a giant conger eel is hooked.

But at the outset, each budding sea angler has to resolve a basic question: does he wish to fish afloat or from the shore? Most experienced sea anglers do both but the beginner, starting from scratch and with all the tackle to buy, is advised to restrict himself for a time to one or the other.

Shore fishing is perhaps more difficult but less expensive in the long term. Boat fishing costs money every time the angler puts to sea but the sea shore is free fishing. Individual choice must decide which to start with but it is probably right to suggest that anglers who fish the North Sea shore, including Kent and Sussex, have better shore fishing available to them. Devon

Rocky areas are often hot spots for most species of sea fish but extreme care should be taken on these dangerous marks.

and Cornwall and parts of Wales and Scotland also fish to a high standard from the shore but boat fishing is frequently the most rewarding in areas where the availability of harbours makes this possible.

Boat fishing has the advantage that in its simplest form, it merely requires a baited hook to be sunk to the seabed.

An absolute novice is therefore always more likely to catch fish from a boat than from the shore.

The best advice for anyone new to sea angling is to become involved in your local club. There is one, be assured of that – even towns a long way from the coast now have thriving sea fishing associations who organise regular trips. Many clubs pride themselves on the help they give newcomers of all ages. Knowledge, as always, is the key to success and it is a slow process to try to teach yourself. Books help but there is no substitute for becoming involved at club level.

Let's have a look at the tackle you need. Continued on page 54

Boat fishing needs a certain amount of brute force to heave big fish off the bottom, so hefty tackle is needed.

SHORE

Rod: While fish, especially bass, can be caught only a few yards into the surf while shore fishing, generally the best rewards fall to anglers who can make long casts – up to 150 yards – to reach the deeper water. To enable you to achieve this a powerful rod is obviously needed. Brute force will not gain the maximum distance. You must get the rod to do the work for you, timing your cast. The longer the rod the further the lead and bait will be cast.

There are three main types of shore rods – called beach casters – available. Ones with reverse taper, medium fast taper and stiff butt with a very fast tip. I would recommend the medium fast for beginners as it will cope with most angling needs. Choose one between 10ft and 11ft which is capable of casting lead weights of 3oz–6oz. When buying the rod make sure it feels comfortable, is made of hollow fibre glass and the rod rings and fittings are of good quality for they will have to stand up against the corrosive factors of the sea. Solid glass rods are unsuitable for beach casting but if you decide you just want to fish from rocks, jetties or piers, then these cheaper models will cope.

Reel: Big fixed spool reels can be used for beach casting but I prefer multipliers. While fixed spool reels are easier for the beginner to come to terms with than multipliers, the latter, once mastered, are far superior. When buying any sea reel make sure the spools are wide and shallow, capable of carrying at least 200 yards of 20lb line.

If you want to use a fixed spool reel for beach casting it should be the large model.

A light spinning rod can give tremendous fun when after mackerel.

Fixed spool

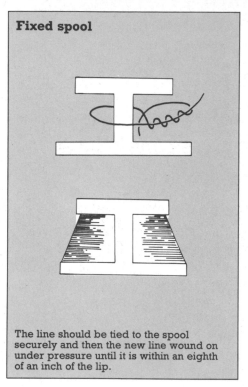

The line should be tied to the spool securely and then the new line wound on under pressure until it is within an eighth of an inch of the lip.

Multipliers

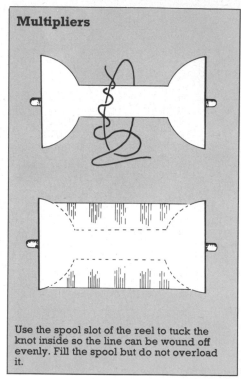

Use the spool slot of the reel to tuck the knot inside so the line can be wound off evenly. Fill the spool but do not overload it.

Line: Remember you are casting heavy weights so the line you put on the reel needs to be strong enough to cope with the shock of casting a big lead out.

Lines of 12lb breaking strain can easily be snapped on the cast with the force of the lead weight. If you are fishing at distance the strike needs to be a powerful one to ensure the fish is well hooked.

The disadvantage of using a heavy line is that the swell of the sea will form a big bow in the line which at times will make bite detection difficult. Also with heavier gear the distances you can achieve when beach casting are restricted because as the line starts to run off the spool during a cast it will slow the cast down as it rubs the sides of the spool

Lighter lines of between 10lb and 15lb can be used providing a casting leader *(see diagram)* is attached to the business end of the tackle. Known as a shock absorber, this line should be around 35lb and about 15ft long. The reel line is tied on to it so that when the cast is made the heavier line takes the initial impact before the lead is punched out to sea.

Rod rests: When fishing off piers, rocks or jetties there is usually something on which you can stand your rod, but on the beach you need a rest. It is best if you can hold your rod throughout but this does become tiring. Rod rests should be the tripod type which can be stood easily on sand or shingle beaches. These can be either bought or made.

An end to a good days fishing and the young anglers decide to weigh their biggest wrasse.

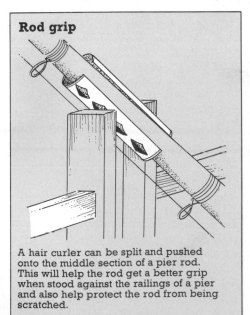

Rod grip

A hair curler can be split and pushed onto the middle section of a pier rod. This will help the rod get a better grip when stood against the railings of a pier and also help protect the rod from being scratched.

Lug and rag worms are good baits for flatfish but mounted on a flounder spoon (bottom right) they are more effective.

Leads: The casting weights you will need will vary according to the area you are fishing. If the tide runs are strong you will need a heavier lead to hold bottom than on a slack tide. On beaches with few underwater obstructions such as rocks, the grapnel or breakaway leads are favourite, for they will grip the bottom. The torpedo type leads are ideal when there is a slow tide flow or when fishing over rough ground. The sizes you carry should be between 3oz and 6oz. If the rod you have chosen casts a maximum of 6oz do not try to overload the action by tying on a lead of 8oz.

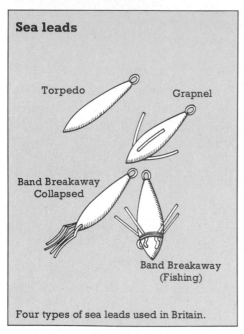

Sea leads

Torpedo

Grapnel

Band Breakaway
Collapsed

Band Breakaway
(Fishing)

Four types of sea leads used in Britain.

Hooks: The sizes you use will depend very much on the bait you fish with and the size of the fish you are seeking. Cod fishing requires a big bait and a large hook, firstly to get the bait on comfortably and second to make sure the fish is hooked – for cod have very large mouths. Flatfish will require a smaller bait and a smaller hook since their mouths are nowhere near as big.

For cod fishing, hooks of around 4/0 will catch both 2lb fish and ones of 20lb, while for dab and plaice fishing size six long shank hooks are ideal when fishing with a single lugworm or ragworm. When buying the bigger hooks make sure they are forged for greater strength. All the hooks must be eyed models.

Traces: As in coarse fishing, your trace should be slightly weaker than your reel line in case you snag on the bottom. Booms on which to tie your traces can be bought but I prefer the

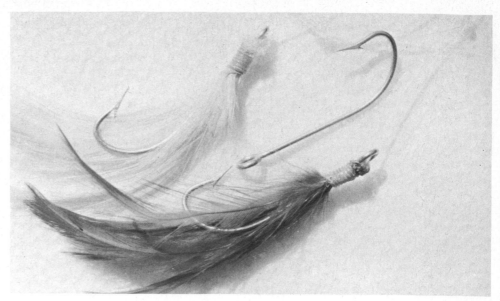

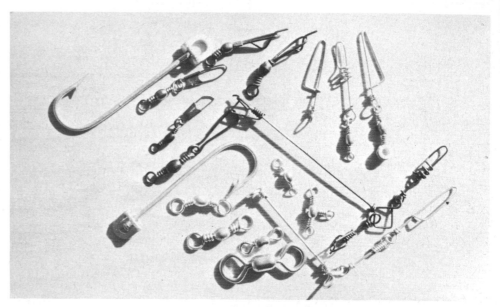

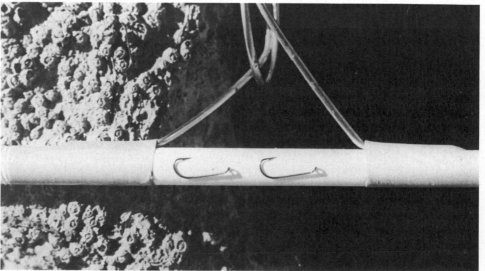

Top to bottom:
The tackle you are likely to need – mackerel feathers, especially when boat fishing.
A selection of swivels and booms.
An assortment of hooks including these smaller ones for mullet fishing.

basic paternoster or the running leger set-ups (see diagrams).

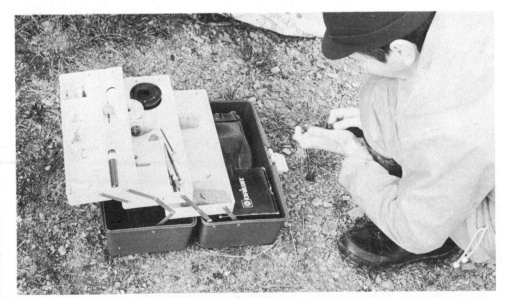

Top to bottom:
A few floats are always handy when fishing from rocks or piers.
Pirks will normally catch cod, pollack and ling.
A sturdy tackle box to house all these accessories.

Common set-up

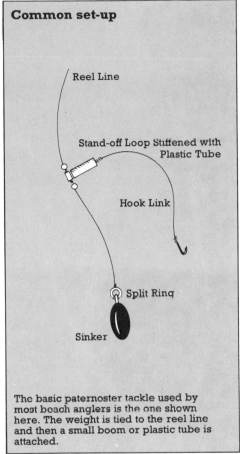

Reel Line

Stand-off Loop Stiffened with Plastic Tube

Hook Link

Split Ring

Sinker

The basic paternoster tackle used by most beach anglers is the one shown here. The weight is tied to the reel line and then a small boom or plastic tube is attached.

Swivels: A few in each size will always come in handy. Buy the snap swivel which can be tied on the line and the lead weight attached to it. Should the tide run increase, a bigger weight can be put on the line in seconds. The standard swivels are useful to stop the line from kinking.

Swivels

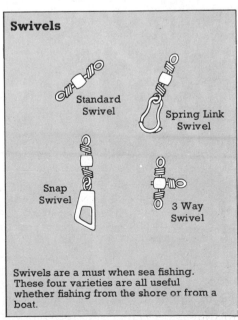

Standard Swivel

Spring Link Swivel

Snap Swivel

3 Way Swivel

Swivels are a must when sea fishing. These four varieties are all useful whether fishing from the shore or from a boat.

On the run

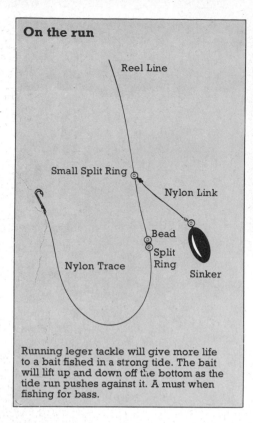

Reel Line

Small Split Ring

Nylon Link

Bead

Split Ring

Nylon Trace

Sinker

Running leger tackle will give more life to a bait fished in a strong tide. The bait will lift up and down off the bottom as the tide run pushes against it. A must when fishing for bass.

Accessories: There is no real need for a basket. All the kit can be carried in a small canvas bag. Take a light-weight folding stool if you are beach fishing because standing up for several hours becomes tiring. You will always find a use for pliers and a sharp knife. Keep all your hooks and swivels in plastic boxes and don't allow the rain or saltwater to get into them since this will cause the hooks and swivels to rust and therefore weaken them.

Float-fishing

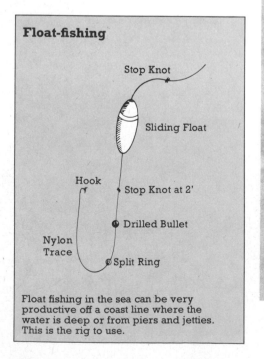

Stop Knot

Sliding Float

Hook

Stop Knot at 2'

Drilled Bullet

Nylon Trace

Split Ring

Float fishing in the sea can be very productive off a coast line where the water is deep or from piers and jetties. This is the rig to use.

Two anglers cast into the foaming surf after bass. When fishing for bass man or third breaker.

nglers make the mistake of casting too far. These fish will feed very close to the shore – along the line of the second

BOAT

Rod: While it costs more to go boat fishing, per trip, the kit you need is very simple. Because no casting is involved – you are merely lowering the bait over the side – you need only a rod of about 6ft – 8ft in length. Solid glass is as good for this type of fishing as hollow glass. It needs to be sturdy because the weights and the size of fish you can expect to catch will be very much larger than when beach fishing. Again the rod rings should be tough – the more expensive models have roller rings on them to help protect the line when "pumping" fish up from the bottom. "Pumping" is the term used for playing big fish. If a large fish is hooked it is impossible to reel it straight in. You have to lift the rod up as far as possible to gain some line, wind the line on to the reel as you lower the rod back down into position and then repeat the process until the fish is on the surface.

Reels: Fixed spool reels are not practical for boat fishing. A strong multiplier or a simple centre-pin (the drum type reel) is ideal. They should be loaded with something like 50lb line for deep sea fishing where big cod, ling and conger are always a possibility. When boat fishing, say, a few hundred yards offshore then the line can be decreased slightly.

A level wind multiplier is by far the best reel when boat fishing.

Weights: The size of the lead weights you will need to carry really depends on where you will be fishing. It is best to have a word with your local tackle dealer or the skipper of the boat before setting out. Find out how strong the tides are and what sort of depth of water you are likely to be fishing over. These factors will dictate the size of the lead – but in some instances as much as 1lb of lead is needed to hold your bait on the bottom.

A 32lb ling is safely aboard. This is the size of fish you can expect when wreck fishing.

Artificial sand eels are a deadly bait for big pollack like this 21lb specimen. When a shoal of pollack are found it can mean a fish a cast.

Pirks: These are heavy metal type spinners. They are lowered to the bottom and then jigged up and down in the hope of fish such as cod, pollack, haddock or ling mistaking them for small fish. In recent years they have accounted for many good catches but they are fairly expensive to buy, especially since the chances are that a few will be lost if the bottom is snaggy.

Hooks: Concentrate on the larger sizes although a few smaller models do come in handy, especially if you fish for sea bream or whiting.

In both forms of fishing, make sure you have water proof clothing with you and in the colder months wrap up well. If you fish from a boat during the summer take a couple of jumpers with you just in case. It may look like a boiling hot day but once you are out on the ocean it can turn mighty cold. There is nothing worse than having to spend the day shivering. It won't do you any good and your fishing will certainly suffer because you will be more occupied with trying to keep warm than catching fish.

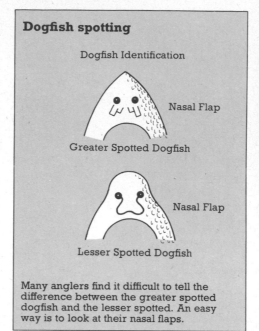

Dogfish spotting

Dogfish Identification

Nasal Flap

Greater Spotted Dogfish

Nasal Flap

Lesser Spotted Dogfish

Many anglers find it difficult to tell the difference between the greater spotted dogfish and the lesser spotted. An easy way is to look at their nasal flaps.

Sea hints

Although mackerel feathers are cheap they are also very easy to make. Long bright feathers can be tied onto a bare hook in seconds if the four sequences are followed:

For making a stand off loop in your line – for use in conjunction with a plastic boom – use the following knot. Coupled with the boom it will help keep the baited hook off the line.

Lugworm, the most popular bait, need to be mounted on the hook carefully. Worms should be placed on the hook by threading the hook right down the middle of the body tube.

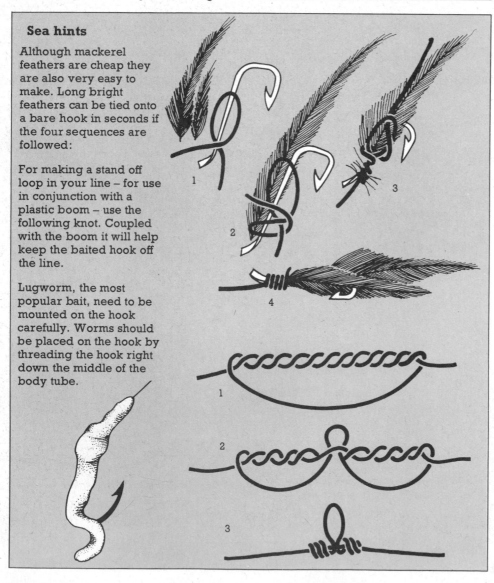

A large pollack swung overboard afte

...ing safely gaffed by the skipper. This fish fell to legered mackerel strip – a bait that will attract most species.

CHAPTER TWELVE

Sea baits – collect your own

When it comes to bait, sea anglers are far luckier than coarse fishermen. With a little effort they can collect all the bait they need for a day's fishing – completely free.

Some anglers rely on tackle shops for their bait, especially if they live a long way from the coast but anglers who live near the sea have the chance to dig or collect their own supplies. The variety of bait which can be used to catch sea fish is almost endless but let's first deal with the five most popular ones; those which are used throughout the country all the year round.

Lugworms: These sluggish worms, which are found on sand or sand/mud flats at low water, are the most widely used bait for while they are easy to dig they will also attract almost every form of sea fish that swims. They are a must when cod fishing but will be equally effective when fishing for flat-fish, whiting or bass.

They are found throughout the British Isles wherever there is a sandy or muddy beach. The way to collect them is to go to the beach armed with a garden fork, at low tide and look for their "casts". These are spaghetti shaped rings of sand which lie on the surface. They are caused by the worm excreting the sand through its body after having eaten the tiny organisms found in it. Not far away from the cast is what is called the "blow hole" – a small depression in the sand where the worm will eventually end up after it has eaten its way through the rest of the sand. Lugworm burrows are almost always U shaped, and the worm always faces towards the blow hole. Take the fork and place the prongs about nine inches away from the line between the blow hole and the cast and push the fork into the sand to a depth of about a foot. Take out the fork full of sand and turn it over with a quick flick of the wrist. You should quickly spot the worm – which has a plump cylindrical body tapering off to a thin tail which contains sand. If you cannot see it, search through the dug out sand carefully until it is found.

Sometimes the lugworm will be

The beauty with sea fishing is you can collect your own bait – providing you know what to look for.

further down in the sand but usually a foot is plenty deep enough to dig. Lugworm are usually found in ones but where they are plentiful you can often dig up three worms in one go.

If you are going to use the worms straight away they can be placed in a normal plastic bait tin but if you want to store them for several days then they must be looked after carefully. In hot weather lugworm will go off quickly and become useless as bait – they will turn into a mess of blood and skin if not stored in a cool place. The garage floor is ideal. Place them in layers of clean newspaper but don't overcrowd them. Put them in rows about an inch apart and then place them in a wooden box – a seed box is just the job. Change the paper when the worms start letting out some of their juices. Even with this careful nursing, lugworm will only stay fresh for about three days.

Ragworm: Another very popular bait which will catch most species of fish. It looks very similar to a fat centipede and can be found in a variety of different habitats, but they tend to be most prolific on muddy beaches or harbours and areas of mixed mud and gravel. Unlike the obliging lugworm, the rag leaves no tell-tale cast so when you go digging for him it is a matter of trial and error. Keep digging until you come across a batch of ragworm and then work the area carefully. There are several different kinds of ragworm but the two most common are the small harbour rag which make perfect bait for mullet and flat-fish fishing and the king rag which is greenish and can grow up to 18 inches in length. These are perfect for all forms of fishing.

The bigger king rag can be found on beaches where there are a lot of boulders. Turn one of the big stones over quickly and there's a good chance a big juicy worm will be hiding under it – but grab it quickly before it burrows back into the sand. Obviously ragworm can only be dug, like lugworm, at low tide.

They keep better than lugworm and should be stored in a wooden tray containing a layer of newspaper on which should be placed a layer of damp, gravelly sand. When baiting up with ragworm be careful of its pincers which can give you an unexpected bite. Hold the worm firmly by the head before pushing it on to the hook.

Crabs: The crab which makes the most succulent of all sea baits is the "peeler" or "soft-backed" crab. These two crabs are the same as the common beach crabs you find along the sea shore but have reached a stage of their lives when they have outgrown their shell and are about to replace it with a bigger one. The peeler is when the crab is at the stage of discarding his old shell and the soft backed is when the shell has been done away with

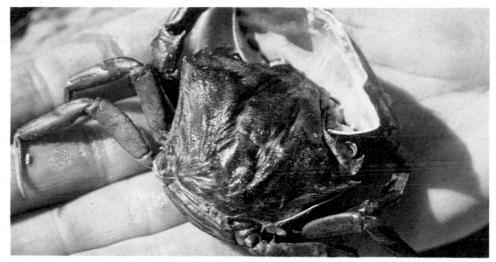
Peeler crabs, although not easy to find, are great for cod, bass and flounders.

A lugworm – a bait which will catch all sea fish. It is easy to spot by the cast (right) which it leaves on the surface.

and a new, soft velvety shell has taken its place.

The soft-backed crab is easy to spot but because it has lost its shell – and therefore its protection – it will hide away in nooks and crannies until the new shell has hardened. So when you go looking for soft-backs along a rocky coast line take a small metal rod bent into the shape of a hook at the end. This can be used to poke around the crevices in search of these creatures which make excellent bait for bass, flounders, cod and pollack.

The peeler crab is more difficult to spot because it is still carrying its old shell. Look for them in sheltered estuaries, enclosed bays or creeks where there are rocks and areas of mud or sand, and also in any crevices which may be about. But how do you spot a peeler? If you see a crab clasping another to its stomach you can be sure that the one on the abdomen is a female peeler or softback, being protected until she has grown a new shell.

The surest way is to break off one of the crabs legs close to the joint. If bits of tendon are attached it is a hardback crab but if it comes off cleanly like a boot it is a peeler. This test will not bother the crab too much because at the next moult it will grow a new leg. Peelers and soft-back should be collected in a bucket and then transferred to a wooden or plastic container containing freshly gathered seaweed and stored in a cool outhouse. They can be kept for several days but softbacks should be used quickly before they grow a hard shell. June and July are the best months for collecting these baits.

When mounting these crabs on to a hook, break off the claws and on peelers, the old shell. Break off a leg where it joins the body and insert the hook through the hole where the leg used to be and then through the crab's fleshy back. To make sure it stays firmly on the hook during a long cast,

Hermit crabs are not so common as peeler and hardbacks but if found make a succulent bait.

some thin cotton can be wound around the crab and the hook shank.

Mussels: A bait which many anglers swear by when they go fishing for cod, haddock or wrasse. It is a bait I have never had much success with but I know that cod anglers on the Yorkshire coast use them as much as lugworm. They are a good standby bait when you are unable to get a supply of lug or rag. Mussels can be found clinging to rocks, harbour walls or pier piles. Once collected, the mussel has to be removed from its hard shell. This is done by pushing a short bladed knife into where the two halves of the shell are joined and working it along the mussel until you are able to prise it open. The meat inside can then be taken out after cutting the leathery hinge which holds it in its shell. When

baiting up place the hook into the black "tongue" which is found on mussels. This will ensure the mussel is firmly on the hook. Two or three can be

Mussels can be found clinging to rocks and stones in estuaries.

Crabs will take shelter under old pots or tins left in the mud at low tide.

Turbot, like this 11lb fish, are one of Britain's largest flatfish. They are most common around Cornwall and Devon.

placed on to one hook when fishing for cod.

Fish baits: Another of the popular baits which will catch fish all around Britain's coast. It is a must when deep sea fishing for ling, pollack or conger and equally effective when shore fishing for cod, flat-fish, and thornback.

The two most popular fish used as bait are mackerel and herring. When placed on the hook they emit an oily scent trail which attracts fish. Obviously the size of the fish you are seeking will dictate the size of the piece of fish used as bait. This is something many beginners seem to forget. They put on great big pieces of fish, forgetting that the flounders or dabs they are after haven't got big enough mouths to eat the offering. Likewise, if you are after big specimens like thornback, cod or ling, the offering needs to be man-sized. However big your bait needs to be, the first step when using fish baits is to cut the herring or mackerel into two fillets. This is done by running a very sharp knife along the side of the fish, from its head to its tail, making sure you cut close to the bone.

You should now have two slender, triangular shaped fillets. One fillet will be just the job, mounted on a big hook when fishing for conger. When you are after smaller fish cut the fillets into strips. For fish such as cod, thornbacks or ling cut the fillet lengthways so you get two strips – use one of these long strips as bait. For flat-fish or whiting and other similar, smaller fish, cut the fillet into half inch wide strips, making sure you run the knife at an angle across the fillet from its back to its belly. The strip should end up slightly longer than the width of the fillet. The hook should be pushed through the fleshy part of the strip, near the top, and then pushed through again into the skin. This will make it hang attractively in the water. When using fish strips or whole fillet a flowing trace is best so that the bait is given an appealing movement as it flutters on the bottom with the pull of the tide. If you are missing bites and only part of the fish strip has been chewed, it is worth making the bait smaller.

The five baits I have mentioned will be adequate for most situations and fish you are likely to encounter. There are many other baits which can be used such as squid (excellent for cod and bass), shrimps, sandeels (a very good bass bait if fished with alive), cockles, razor fish and cuttlefish. These

How to fillet a mackerel.
Take a sharp knife and cut along the backbone.
Separate both sides.
Both fillets can be used if after big fish but it's best to cut them into smaller strips.

are baits you can try out once you have become accustomed to handling your tackle and catching a few fish on the baits mentioned in detail. To start with I would recommend using either lugworm or ragworm as these will attract most species of fish and will at least give a chance of hooking into something early in your sea fishing career.

Remember that with all baits you use, try and make them look as appealing and natural as possible. Thread lugworms and ragworms on to the hook carefully. If the hook is not completely covered after one worm has been placed on it slide another on until only the point of the hook is showing.

Continued on page 70

The beauty of the flounder is it can be caught the whole year round from the beach, boat or estuaries.

Artificial baits: The only artificial baits I would recommend are spinners, pirks and imitation sandeels. The pre-packed baits which can be bought are nowhere near as effective as fresh bait and should only be used in emergencies. Pirks and sandeel imitations are fished only off boats for cod, ling or pollack.

Spinning, used to simulate a small fish swimming through the water, can be very effective from the shore, especially during the summer from jetties, piers, harbour walls and rocks where you are likely to get stuck into shoals of mackerel or the long, slender garfish. Use the toby type of spinner coupled with a spinning rod and line of about 5lb to give you the maximum casting distance and best sport from these fish. There is always the possibility of a bonus bass or pollack on this method. After casting it out as far as possible let it sink for a few seconds before starting the retrieve. Keep on casting until you locate a shoal of fish.

Fresh sandeels are one of the best baits for bass.

This assortment of spinners should be ample for both rock and dingy fishing.

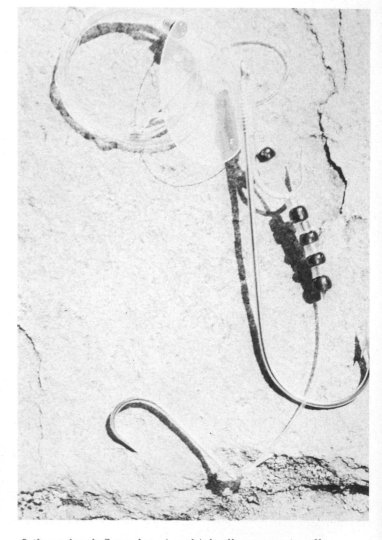

A three hook flounder rig which allows you to offer more than one choice of bait.

This youngster has every reason to look happy – and who wouldn't with a pollack of this size. This fish was caught from Mevagissey, Cornwall.

CHAPTER THIRTEEN

Know your sea fish

The brightly coloured wrasse can be found around most rocky marks in the South West.

There are scores of different sea fish swimming around the British coast so it would be impossible to list them all for identification purposes. But the following are the ones you are most likely to encounter. All records are for shore fishing.

BASS *(Dicentrachus labrax)*
Record, 18lb 2oz.
Identification: The most sporting fish to be found around the British coastline. It is a muscular powerful fish with a mass of silvery scales. The dorsal fin is spiney, similar to that of a perch. The mouth is big to enable it to feed on a variety of baits.
Location: The bass is not widespread. Most of the bass catches are made south of the Wash, right down to Cornwall and back up the Cornish coastline to Wales. Some of the best bass grounds are in Essex, the Isle of Wight and the surf beaches around St. Ives, Cornwall.
Feeding habits and baits: They appear in their greatest numbers between March and October and when they are really feeding will take anything thrown at them with a bang. They can be the perfect fish for a novice because when they patrol beaches they can often be caught less than 30 yards from the shoreline. They seem to prefer swimming in the undertow of the surf, routing around for food. Fish strip, lug and ragworm and peeler crab are all good baits but the most effective is live or dead sandeel. When a bass takes the bait, even a fish of around 2lb, it will usually wallop the rod round.

BREAM (Anglers are concerned with two types of sea bream – red and black.)
The red bream *(Pagellus bogaraveo)*
Record, 3lb.
This is a super little fighter. Fish of up to 9½lb have been caught from boats but the larger specimens rarely come inshore. The body is varying shades of red, the lower flanks and belly are pink and the fish has huge eyes which look almost out of proportion with its body. It has a large mouth full of needle sharp teeth.
Location: Red bream are concentrated in the South of England mainly around the Cornish coast where they show in great numbers during the summer.
Feeding habits and bait: The bigger fish prefer to remain in deep water so boat fishing is the only way to catch them.
The smaller samples of around 1lb will come in close to the shore. They are not too fussy what they eat but fish strip is as good a bait as any, especially strips cut from a fresh mackerel.

Black Bream *(spondyliosoma cantharus)*
Record, 4lb 14¼oz.
This fish is not black but has a dark appearance. Its body is a bluish grey and it is much dumpier than the red bream. It has dark striping across its back and the same large eyes as the red bream.
Location: These fish are concentrated more at the Eastern end of the Channel especially around the Sussex coast. They arrive around the end of April and disappear in late summer.
Feeding habits and baits: Black bream rarely venture very close to the shore so fishing from a boat is essential if you want to catch these lively fighters. Like red bream they will take most baits. When baiting up make sure it is secure, for bream have a habit of being able to nibble away at the bait without being hooked.

COD *(gadus morhua)*
Record, 44½lb.
Identification: The cod is the most sought after fish in Britain. The bigger fish tend to have huge, dropping bellies, and all cod have large heads in

Mullet can be fished for with coarse tackle in harbours and around piers. Bread is a good bait.

proportion to their bodies. Their mouths can look like giant crevaces, which is why anglers use large baits and hooks when after cod. They have a small "beard" underneath their chin and have a mustardy pattern running along their backs and flanks. Their belly is normally white but can be a reddish colour if caught over rocky ground.

Location: The reason cod are so popular is that they are found off almost all Britain's coastline from the shore and boats. While cod can be caught all the year round, the best times are during the colder months from autumn to early spring.

Feeding habits and baits: For most of the year cod stocks stay well off shore but as the weather turns cooler around September they start to move in. Fishing from the shore is better at night when cod will feed more freely. Tides are very important when cod fishing, with most fish being caught at high tide.

Lugworm are the best all round cod bait but because of the size of the fish's mouth the worm should be threaded

All mine. This youngster is dwarfed by the 54lb conger he landed single handed while wreck fishing.

on to a large hook in bunches to make them more appetising. If you are using fairly small worms then as many as five may be needed to fill the hook. With the very large worms you can get away with just one or two on the hook. When fishing for cod, wait for a positive bite – the fish will usually swallow the bait.

CONGER *(Conger conger)*
Record, 67lb 1oz.
Identification: The conger looks just like a giant eel. The above weight is for the shore-caught record but the boat-caught biggest is a staggering 109lb 6oz.
Location: They are found mainly off Dorset, South Devon and Cornwall and while the smaller fish can be caught from rocky marks inshore the best catches come from boats which take anglers to fish over war-time wrecks. These big fish will hang around wrecks waiting for food to come along with the tide.
Feeding habits and bait: Conger can be caught all the year round but fishing is best during the summer months. Conger prefer to lie and wait

for the bait to come to them so fishing from a drifting boat, where you are constantly covering new ground, is most rewarding. Half sides of mackerel or herring or big pieces of squid are the most successful baits.

DAB (Limanda limanda)
Record, 2lb 9½oz.

Identification: The dab is a member of the flat-fish family. Its back is a sandy colour and underneath it is white. Like all flat fish both of its eyes are on the same side of its body – looking up towards the surface. Dabs have no outstanding markings but if they are held up to the light you can almost see right through them.

Location: Dabs are found in no shortage all along the coast. They favour sandy, muddy ground and can be caught quite easily from piers, beaches, and harbours. Dabs of 1lb can be classed as an excellent catch but while they do not grow very big or fight much when hooked they do make excellent eating.

Feeding habits and bait: Like all flat-fish, they feed mainly on the bottom. The baits used – lugworm, ragworm and small strips of fish – should be kept on the small side because dabs have small mouths.

DOGFISH; LESSER SPOTTED (Scyliorhinus canicula)
Record, 4½lb.

Identification: A sleek, predatory fish with a mild resemblance to the shark. It is, in fact, the smallest member of the shark family. It is covered in brown spots, has a long, streamlined tail and small beady eyes. Its skin is as rough as sandpaper so be very careful when handling it – it can rasp your skin.

Location: While dogfish are easy to catch when you drop on a shoal, put up little fight and are not particularly good for eating, they can be caught from most areas in Britain.

Feeding habits and bait: Dogfish can be caught at all levels and often intercept a bait which is intended for other fish. Best bait is fish strip or squid.

FLOUNDER (Platichthys flesus)
Record, 4lb 7oz.

Identification: A very obliging member of the flat-fish family which will feed all the year round and provide you with sport when otherwise you may catch nothing.

Its back is dark brown and the underneath of the fish is white. If you run your finger from its tail to its head you will feel it has very rough skin.

Location: Found in estuaries, harbours and off beaches and rocky areas all along the British coastline. Can be caught all the year round but feeds best during the winter months until January when they move off to the deeper water to spawn.

Feeding habits and bait: Most of the bigger specimens are caught in estuaries and take a variety of baits ranging from peeler crab to lugworm and fish strips. They will accept anything and the size of the bait is not that important – they have big appetites. If you are using a big bait, give the fish plenty of time to take it properly before striking.

HADDOCK (Melanogrammus aeglefinus)
Record, 6lb 12oz.

Identification: The haddock is closely related to the cod and looks similar. While it is smaller, it has the same small beard under its chin but it can be distinguished from a cod by its forked tail and distinctive dark patch on each shoulder.

Location: They rarely venture close enough to the shoreline to make it worthwhile fishing for them from beaches. Boat anglers, however, have great sport with them

They are common around the Scottish coast but the only other two areas worth fishing for them are Yorkshire and Cornwall.

Feeding habits and bait: Haddock are mainly bottom feeders with a very varied diet. They will feed on razor fish, whelks, worms, squid and shrimps so obviously all these baits are worth trying when setting out for haddock. Haddock swim around in shoals so if you catch one, its odds-on there will be more to follow. They are excellent to eat, especially when smoked.

LING (Molva molva)
Record, 15lb 5oz.

Identification: Another member of the cod family but much more streamlined. While its head resembles that of a cod its body looks more like that of a conger eel. The boat record is 57lb but even these big fish do not put up much of a fight when hooked. It is really a case of brute force to get them to the surface.

Location: Most ling are caught from boats over the same marks used for conger fishing. Ling will swim around the same wrecks looking for food and will often intercept a bait

The thick lips of the wrasse make it easy to identify. These two fish were tempted with peeler crab fished only yards from the shore.

before the conger get to it. The biggest concentration of ling are found off Devon and Cornwall and in Scottish waters.

Feeding habits and bait: Like the conger they feed on the bottom in deep water. They are shoal fish and once a skipper has located them it is not uncommon for a party of anglers to take as many as 2,000lb of these fish in one outing. The average size being between 18lb and 25lb. They are big fish so a big bait is needed – half or a quarter of mackerel fillet is as good as any.

MACKEREL *(Scomber scomber)*
Record, 4lb.

Identification: The mackerel has been compared to a torpedo because of its round streamlined body which tapers away from nose to tail. The distinctive colouring is on the back where wavy black bands run down its greenish blue body. The belly is grey to silver.

Location: These fish are widely distributed throughout Britain and can be caught from both boats and inshore, from rocks, piers, beaches and harbour walls. Mackerel, like many other fish, move into our waters in the summer. They usually arrive around June and, once the colder months come, swim into the deep water many miles offshore.

Feeding habits and bait: Mackerel can be called the suicide sea fish for once a shoal has been located they will grab at anything – even a bare hook. Most anglers fish for mackerel purely for bait for other fish such as

conger, ling, and shark. When catching mackerel for bait, a trace of feathers (hooks with coloured feathers tied on) is attached to the reel line and jigged up and down in the water. As soon as the trace hits the shoal, the fish will make a grab for the feathers. If a trace with eight feathers is used, it is usual to catch a fish on nearly every hook. But for good sport a light spinning rod with five pound breaking strain line and a small mackerel spinner is ideal. Fish of 1lb will tear through the water once hooked and fight all the way to the side. They can also be caught on float tackle, especially when fishing from piers or harbours, with mackerel or herring strip, as bait.

MULLET *(Chelon labrosus)*
Record, 10lb.

Identification: There are three species of mullet but the most popular is the thick-lipped mullet, another streamlined fish which is covered in thick silvery-grey scales. For its size it has a very small mouth compared to other sea fish and therefore baits need to be on the small side.

Location: The fish is most widely distributed in the south and in Wales, the favourite areas being Sussex, Hants, Dorset, Devon and the Mid-Wales coastline. Shore anglers have a much greater chance of catching them because they tend to hang around piers, harbour walls and in estuaries, swimming around moored boats. Anywhere where there is a sewage outfall will be a hot spot for these fish.

Feeding habits and bait: Mullet

Muddy estuaries are a favourite haunt of big flatties like this 2lb 6oz flounder.

tend to feed on things like microscopic algae and other organic matter but can be caught on small pieces of paste, bread flake or harbour ragworm (the small rag). While they can be caught on the bottom the best way is to float fish near to the surface – with coarse fishing tackle. A float rod coupled with a fixed spool reel, 3lb line and a small waggler with a size 12 hook is the perfect rig for these shy biting fish. When playing them be careful not to put too much strain on the fish because it is easy to rip the hook from their soft mouths. They are excellent fish for the pan.

POLLACK *(P. pollachius)*
Record, 16lb.

Identification: This fish can grow to 30lb and fish of 20lb are often landed while wreck fishing over deep water. The boat record is 25lb. They have a very dark back which blends into the silvery-grey flanks. Their mouths are big, full of sharp teeth.

Location: Found along most of Britain close to rocks and reefs. They are predatory fish, feeding on sandeels and small mackerel and herrings. Pollack tend to move from area to area in search of food. They can be caught in large quantities – in one place one day and the next you won't catch a single fish – they have moved to a new home.

Feeding habits and bait: Pollack will grab at anything which resembles a small fish. Metal pirks have accounted for many good catches in the past few years as have slivers of fish. But the Redgill lure, which imitates a sandeel, is a real killer when fished from a boat in a strong tide. At times pollack find the lure irresistable.

Continued on page 78

Whiting normally start moving towards the British coastline from September onwards. On light tackle even fish of only 1lb can put up a good fight.

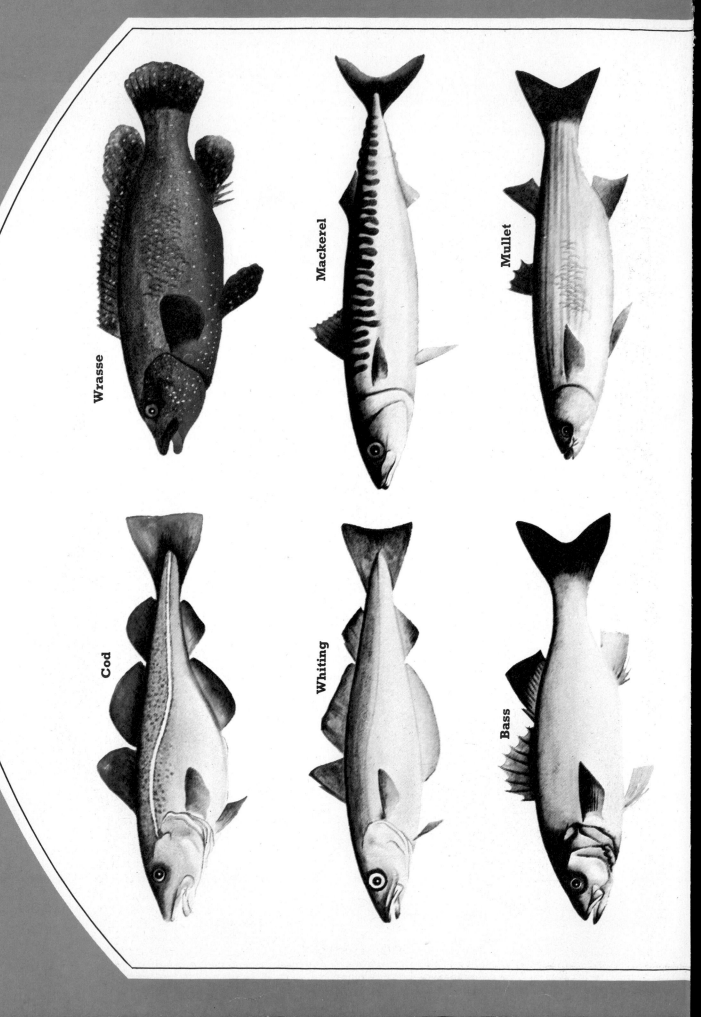

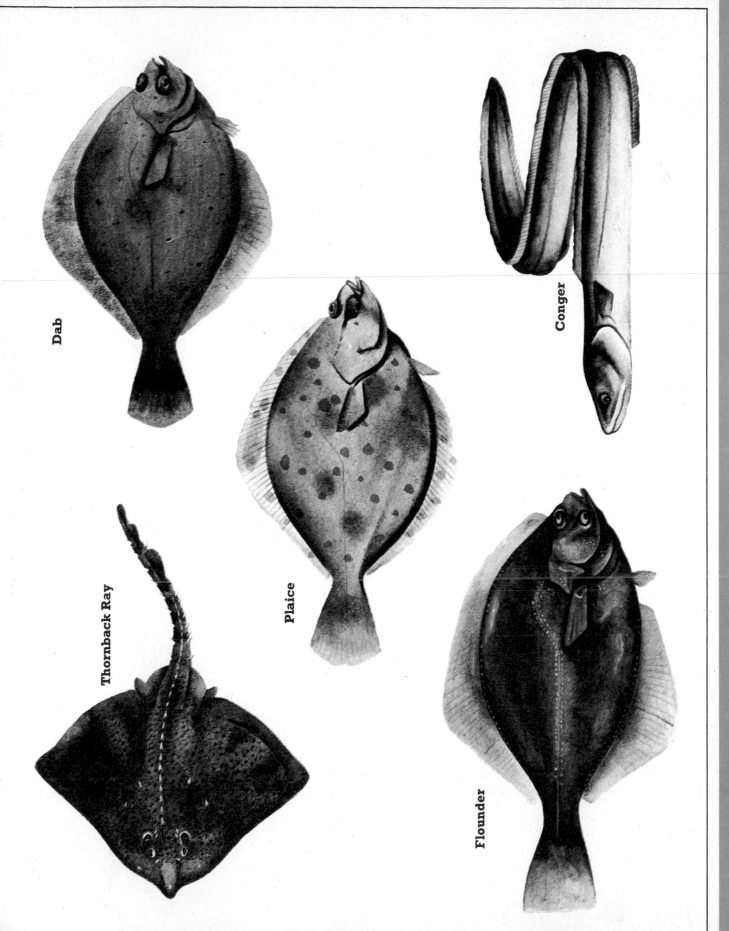

Dab

Conger

Thornback Ray

Plaice

Flounder

SEA FISH

PLAICE (Pleuronectes platessa)
Record, 8lb 1¼oz.

Identification: Yet another flatfish but one which is recognised as the "upper class" of the species. It is an excellent table fish with succulent, soft white meat. Plaice can be easily identified from the big red spots on their olive green backs. Their skin is also very smooth.

Location: Widely distributed but most common where there is an abundance of sandy beaches – the environment which suits them most. Bigger fish sometimes choose a huge rocky area so it is a good idea to fish areas where the sandy bottom eventually meets rocky ground. You have a chance of catching the bigger fish then.

Feeding habits and baits: Like all flatties, fishing on the bottom is best. Boat fishing in shallow inshore marks is often most productive but plenty of fish are caught each year from beaches and piers. The most popular rig is a three hook flowing trace, baited with either lug, ragworm or fish strip. Mussels and shrimps are also good on the hook. With a flowing trace movement is given to the bait which makes it more attractive to plaice, for they are curious fish.

RAY, THORNBACK (Raja clavata)
Record, 19lb.

Identification: There are several different species of ray or skate but the most sought after is the thornback ray. It is a big fish with "wings", and lives on the bottom like all flat-fish. It has a pointed snout and a line of spines along its back and tail. When a bait is fished on the bottom a thornback will often come along and flap on it, suck in the bait and all that will be registered is a series of gentle taps.

Location: The thornback ray are found along most of Britain's coastline but areas of sand or shingle are the best. Wales is an excellent area and so is Cornwall. It is basically a summer species but catches can be made in the spring.

Feeding habits and bait: When hooked thornbacks can put up quite a tussle when they dig their wings into the bottom. They feed mainly on the bottom and it is wise to use a wire trace for they are quite capable of biting through nylon. While boat fishing is most productive many good ray are caught while beach casting. Mackerel fillet is the most popular bait. When using it, the first indications you will get that a ray has approached the bait is a series of small taps – don't strike at them, wait until the fish starts to swim off.

SHARK, BLUE (Prionace glauca)
Record, 75lb (boat 218lb).

Identification: The blue shark is the most common one to be caught from the British coast but there are others – thresher, porbeagle and mako. Threshers grow to around the same size as blue shark but the other two are real heavyweights reaching more than 500lb. As its name implies the blue shark is easily recognised by its colour. The back of the fish is a dark blue, fading into a watery blue on the flanks and finishing with a white or cream belly.

Location: Most blue shark are taken from the West Country – with Looe being one of the main shark fishing ports. Each year hundreds of fish around the 50lb mark are taken. Blue shark are a summer fish; they arrive in British waters around June and then move on in October.

Feeding habits and bait: Shark are usually fished for from boats. A beginner who wants to have a crack at this exciting form of fishing is well advised to go out with a professional skipper. Tackle can be hired and the bait – whole mackerel – are usually caught on the way out to the productive shark grounds.

WHITING (Merlangius merlangus)
Record, 3lb 2oz.

Identification: Whiting are slimmer fish than cod or haddock and have silvery flanks and a greeny, brown back. They are easily identified because they have a dark spot just in front of the shoulders. The head is pointed and the mouth is full of needle sharp teeth.

Location: Whiting are most common in the North Sea and the Channel but can be caught in numbers in many other areas. Mid-Wales has

The thornback ray – when hooked it will hug the bottom with its "wings" Maximum pressure must be used to help land the fish.

become a recognised whiting fishing area.

Feeding habits and bait: Unlike many of the fish we have mentioned which feed best during the summer, whiting move inshore at the first sign of a hard frost. They are normally caught by anglers fishing for cod so put up little resistance on heavy tackle. But fished for with lighter gear, they can provide tremendous sport and also make an excellent table fish. The size of shore-caught whiting is normally around the 1lb mark but once a shoal has been located you can take as many as 30 fish in one sitting. Baits are generally the same as you would use for cod fishing but the hook size should be stepped down slightly.

WRASSE, BALLAN (*Labrus bergylta*)
Record, 8lb 6oz.

Identification: The Ballan Wrasse is a beautifully marked fish with mottled flanks of green, brown and turquoise. It has a dorsel fin which runs along most of its back and it has thick rubbery lips around its mouth. It has a row of almost human-shaped teeth which it uses to crush mussels and crabs.

Location: The fish is caught mainly in the summer months and is most prolific around Devon, Cornwall and the Channel Islands. Unlike many other fish, the wrasse is most numerous inshore, preferring the shallower water.

This makes them ideal for the beginner. Even the smaller fish of around 1lb will give a fantastic fight and test the tackle to the limit.

Feeding habits and baits: Wrasse like to swim around shallow, rocky areas looking for mussels and other crustaceans. In the clear waters of the West Coast the wrasse can often be seen swimming around the rocks or jetties. They can be caught on fish strips or lugworm but the best bait is no doubt mussels. They can be fished either with leger tackle or float gear. Float fishing is favoured over rocky ground because there is less danger of losing your tackle. Your hooks need to be very sharp to penetrate the boney mouth of the wrasse on the strike.

Jaws — to catch shark like this big porbeagle you need expensive specialist tackle and plenty of energy. The fight can last several hours.

CHAPTER FOURTEEN

Habitats of sea fish

No stretch of shore-line will contain an equal distribution of fish. Fish will abound in the areas they prefer best – where they have a chance of finding the most food.

Anglers who spend time looking for likely holding spots will stand a much better chance of consistent success than the angler who merely walks to the nearest spot on the beach, plonks down his tackle and begins to fish. He may be lucky that a few fish swim by and grab his bait but more often than not he will be in for a wasted day.

Fishing from charter boats doesn't present these problems because you will be in the hands of the skipper. With the echo sounder on board his boat he will travel to offshore marks known to hold fish and then proceed to locate them with the echo sounder. He will be finding the fish for you.

But when you fish from the shore it is up to you to do your homework. Tides are very important when fishing from the shore. As the tide starts flowing in it will cover an area of sea-bed – the inter-tidal zone – which may be rich in lugworms or shell-fish. Feeding fish will move on to these marks as the tide moves in, they will feed during the high tide and then move out again as the tide ebbs out. Areas where you have spotted numerous lugworm casts will therefore be good places to fish once they are covered by the tide. Look for any channels which may have formed in the sand and cast into them at high tide, for fish will certainly prefer running along a deeper, sandy channel looking for food than in the comparatively shallow water above it.

No coastline contains an equal amount of fish. Look for bays, rocky marks, or gullies which are likely to hold fish.

Fish will also move alongside break-waters, rocks and posts which will harbour mussels and crabs for them to feed on.

Patches of sand between extensive rock formations are normally very good holding spots for flat-fish and they have one other advantage – because of their structure commercial fishermen cannot work them with nets so there is no fear that stocks have been drastically depleted by over-fishing.

Piers are excellent fishing venues since many of them provide you with deep water throughout the day. Even when the tide is out there may still be enough water to make it worthwhile fishing. But a long cast is not always necessary. Bass, mullet and pollack will happily come right up close to the pier's metal supporting structure looking for food. Sometimes it pays just to lower your tackle over the side of the pier rather than casting out.

When fishing from rocks, try to find areas which are deepest. Often you can come across holes or depressions in the rock formation and these spots are bound to hold more fish, for they will provide the fish with shelter and a plentiful supply of food.

When fishing from rocks be safety conscious. Don't go and perch yourself on a big rock at low tide and stay there as the tide is coming in. You may find yourself cut off with water lapping round you. When climbing about the rocks tread carefully – many rocks have slippery green weed on them which could cause you to break your leg.

As I said, tides play a great role in successful sea fishing. With experience you will be able to learn at which stage of the tides fish will feed best and where they are most likely to be found. Study tide-tables to see when high tide will be and plan to start fishing as the tide begins its inward journey. It is no use getting to the shore as the tide is on its way out for your efforts will be wasted – the fish just won't be there.